Understanding Food Safety Management Systems

– A Practical Approach to the
Application of ISO-22000:2005

ERASMO SALAZAR

To My wife Paula and my children Ana and Eugenio. Traveling so much just makes weekends spent with you all the more precious.

Contents

Foreword

These days, it is crucial for every organization within the food supply chain not only to provide safe foods but also to demonstrate that to interested parties.

The food supply chain is one of the most complex supply chains we have. There is an increasing globalization of food and food ingredients, and the scale of food production is growing fast. Moreover, the world population will reach 9.3 billion people by 2050, which means 2.3 billion more mouths to feed. These developments make the food supply chain a complex network of interacting activities and processes. And to ensure food is safe along this supply chain, organizations must have in place robust food safety management systems to identify, effectively control, and manage the food safety hazards and risks.

The requirements for a food safety management system can be explained in many different ways, but to propose a very generic scheme explaining those requirements for organizations within the food supply chain is a real challenge.

In this book, Erasmo Salazar combines his experience as a food safety assessor, food safety consultant, and quality assurance manager in several food companies with his thorough, concise, and systematic way to evaluate food safety management systems, suggesting a holistic approach in understanding interactions between requirements, communication activities, processes, controls, and resources and proposing an unconventional way to perform the hazard analysis.

Without a doubt this book is an important reference for any professional in the food sector.

Cor Groenveld
Global Head of Food Supply Chain Services, Lloyd's Register
Quality Assurance
Chairman of the Board of the Foundation for
Food Safety Certification

I. – Preface

The ISO-22000:2005 standard seeks to increase the ability of any organization within the food chain to instill confidence that its products will not cause harm to consumers. It is not enough for an organization to feel confident in its own methods; it must be something the organization can prove.

> *This International Standard specifies requirements for a Food Safety Management System where an organization in the food chain needs to demonstrate its ability to control food safety hazards in order to ensure that food is safe at the time of human consumption.*

An organization's top management must be able to visualize the scope of this responsibility when the decision is made to implement an FSMS. The requirements are designed to demonstrate the organization's capability to interested parties such as customers, investors, consumers, and authorities. In other words, the ISO-22000:2005 seeks to protect one of the most important assets of any organization within the food sector: CONFIDENCE.

This book is designed for those in the food sector described as one or more of the following:

- Those wishing to implement ISO-22000:2005 in their workplace in order to certify it
- Those who know the principles of HACCP and want to learn how those principles apply in a management system

- Those who now have a quality management system implemented according to ISO-9001:2008 but lack integration of HACCP
- Those who are auditors or consultants and want to learn the requirements of this standard, how to implement its requirements, and how to audit them

Because it is a management system standard with generic requirements, ISO-22000:2005 can be implemented in any organization within the food chain (e.g., a feed producing organization, a glass bottle manufacturer, an organization that distributes food, a food ingredient manufacturing plant, and so forth).

It is important to note that this book does not contain pre-fabricated manuals and procedures. Instead, the material included is designed to explain the requirements of ISO-22000:2005, without proposing solutions that might not be implemented in some organizations.

Below are acronyms used frequently in the food sector:

- HACCP: Hazard Analysis and Critical Control Point
- FSMS: Food Safety Management System
- CCP: Critical Control Point (including plural)
- PRP: Prerequisite Program (including plural)
- OPRP: Operational Prerequisite Program (including plural)
- QMS: Quality Management System

Understanding the requirements is closely linked with the knowledge and proper use of the terminology included in section 3 of the ISO-22000:2005 and the ISO-9000:2005 standard. In the food sector, many terms are confused or interchanged—for example, "verification" and "validation"; "critical limit" and "acceptable level of the hazard"; or "correction" and "corrective action." It is surprising how many requirements are understood once the terminology is clear. Inside this book, relevant definitions are included to simplify these terms, which are scattered throughout the text in discussions that relate to them.

In the preparation of this book, several documents were used, including draft standards and guidelines, codes of practice, and other notes listed in section nine of this guide. But the most significant contributions have come from dozens of people in audits, workshops, forums, and informal discussions on the subject. I am convinced that both audit and consultancy sessions are exercises of mutual learning.

The ISO-22000:2005 adopts the methodology of the Codex Alimentarius found in the annex of the document CAC-RCP 1, 1969, Rev.4 (2003) "International Code of Practice – General Principles of Food Hygiene" and inserts it into a management system. The word "Codex" refers to this specific document and not to the Codex Alimentarius Commission or any other standard or code of practice published by that committee. The document is free and available at **www.codexalimentarius.net** .

Similarly, and taking into account many readers who have knowledge of the ISO-9001:2008 standard, some common elements will be signaled in the book. Much of this information can be consulted in Annex A of the standard (cross-references to ISO-9001:2008).

The introduction of ISO-22000:2005 reads as follows:

This International Standard specifies the requirements for a Food Safety Management System that combines the following generally recognized key elements to ensure food safety along the food chain, up to the point of final consumption:

— interactive communication;

— management system;

— prerequisite programmes;

— HACCP principles.

Such key elements are represented in the following model:

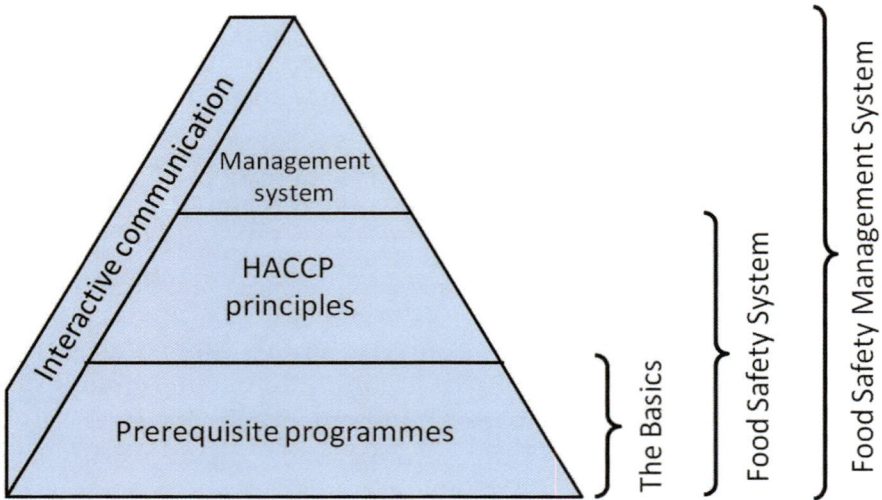

Figure 1 – Food safety management system structure.

While the principles of HACCP and the previous steps to enable hazard analysis included in the Codex do not have any important changes within ISO-22000:2005, there are relevant differences in the applications of these same concepts within the framework of a management system using the cycle PDCA (plan, do, check, act), which is represented in figure 2, adapted from ISO/TS-22004:2005.

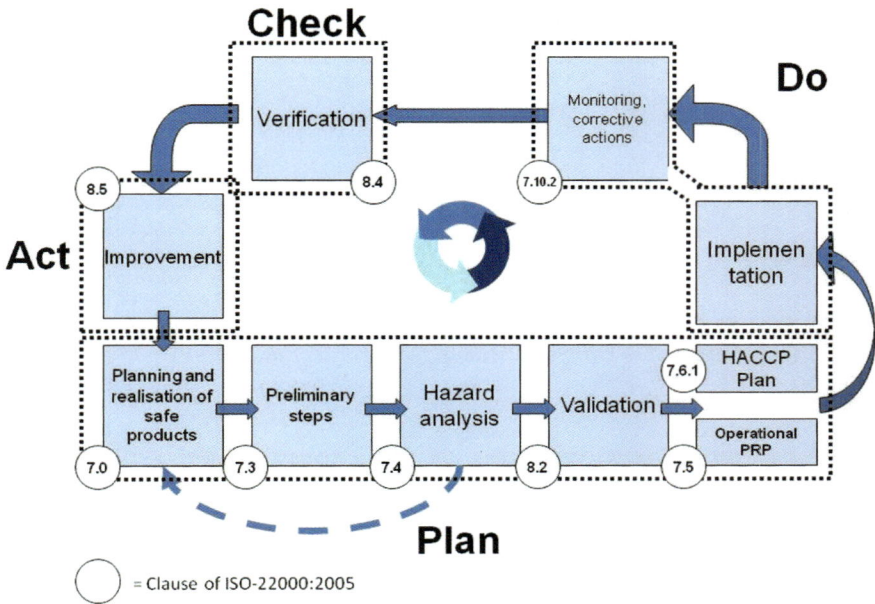

Figure 2 – The concept of continuous improvement
(adapted from ISO/TS-22004:2005).

Given that the management system standards are complex with multiple interdependent requirements, diagrams have been used extensively in this text in order to communicate ideas faster and more thoroughly. Keep in mind that a large part of the comprehension will be obtained when completing the reading of the last section.

This book includes several figures, some of which are adapted from drafts, guides, and other documents. Some, however, are completely new, and "interrelationship diagrams" have been included in order to illustrate the interactions between differing requirements. Taking into account a few simple rules, the idea was borrowed from ISO-9000:2005. Here is an example:

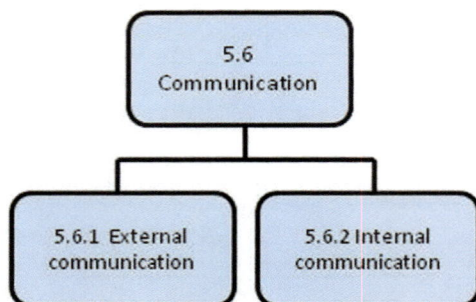

Figure 3 – Interrelationship diagram. Example of partitive relationship between clauses.

Partitive relations between clauses: The clauses in the bottom of figure 3 form a constituent of the upper clause. Clauses 5.6.1 (External communication) and 5.6.2 (Internal communication) are part of clause 5.6 (Communication).

Figure 4 – Interrelationship diagram. Example of direct link relationship between clauses.

Link relations between clauses: Clauses represented with a direct solid line (figure 4) have a clear link to the standard by direct reference to each other. For example, clause 5.6.1 (External communication) is related to clause 5.8.2 (f), as it is part of the input information for management review and has a direct mention in the text of the standard.

Figure 5 – Interrelationship diagram.
Example of associative relationship between clauses.

Inherent relations between clauses: Clauses represented with a dotted line (figure 5) have an implicit relation; in other words, there is no clear reference in the text connecting the clauses; however, both are related. For example, even if there is no direct reference to the standard, 5.6.1 (External communication) is closely related to 7.2.3 (f) (Management of purchased materials), considering the information that should be shared between a supplier and their customers.

Figure 6 – Interrelationship diagram. Example of management system process.

Process relations between clauses: In this example, the arrow represents the flow of management processes. The example illustrated above (figure 6) refers to the result of the verification plan that should be analyzed to comply with 8.4.3 (Analysis of results of verification activities).

Other graphic elements are included in the guide, which facilitate certain concepts and requirements. Below are some examples.

- Quotations from ISO-22000:2005 are shown in italics within a box:

> *The organization shall establish, document, implement and maintain an effective Food Safety Management System and update it when necessary in accordance with the requirements of this International Standard.*

- Quotations from other referenced documents appear in italics:

Where a control measure cannot be validated, it cannot be included within a HACCP plan or in operational PRP, but can be applied within PRP.

- Definitions appear in italics within a divided box. The references are also included:

CCP Critical ControlPoint²	*<Food Safety> step at which control can be applied and is essential to prevent or eliminate a food safety hazard or reduce it to an acceptable level.*

- Links from web pages appear in courier font:

`www.codexalimentarius.net`

Another interesting element emerged a few weeks before the final editing: the inclusion of pictures from different organizations in the food chain. ISO/TS-22003:2007—the specification for certification bodies providing audit and certifications of FSMS—defines thirteen categories, and the best way to illustrate the applicability of the guidance provided in this book in any organization in the food chain is by showing diverse operations. The pictures were provided by friends and colleagues to whom I am thankful.

This book is not intended as a step-by-step guide, which is really not useful in management systems; in fact, readers familiar with the twelve step methodology of the Codex Alimentarius may find this text complicated at first. This book can be likened to those 3D computer-generated images where you must divert your eyes for a moment to concentrate on the larger image. First, it might be difficult to comprehend, but once your brain absorbs the image, the text becomes understandable and very logical.

The requirements of ISO-22000:2005 begin in section four of the standard. Beginning here, the standard ISO-22000:2005 must be read in tandem.

The goal of this text is to demystify ISO-22000:2005 into clear and direct information. Enjoy your read!

Category A Farming 1 (animals). Chicken farm for egg production in Puebla, Mexico. Photo by Jose A Camacho.

2. – List of Figures

3. – List of Tables

4. – Food Safety Management System

> *The organization shall establish, document, implement and maintain an effective Food Safety Management System and update it when necessary in accordance with the requirements of this International Standard.*

Management System [8]	*System to establish policy and objectives and to achieve those objectives.*
Food Safety Management System [16]	*Set of interrelated or interacting elements to establish policy and objectives and to achieve those objectives, used to direct and control an organization with regard to food safety.*

This section includes documentation requirements of the Food Safety Management System (FSMS).

General Requirements (4.1)

To begin implementing or to begin auditing an FSMS, the scope of the management system must be defined. The scope of the system dictates and leaves the same basis for the implementation and its posterior evaluation. The scope consists of the following:

- Products or product categories
- Processes
- Production sites

According to ISO/TS-22003:2007, the certification body will define the scope of certification in terms of levels of the food chain such as primary production, processing, production of packaging material, categories, and sectors. The certification body must not exclude parts of processes, sectors, products, or services from the scope when these influence the food safety of the end product.

Beyond these parameters, it is important to remember that many organizations have outsourced processes that directly impact the conformity of their products. In these cases, it is necessary for the organization to control such processes. This must also be documented within the management system.

The following list includes examples of commonly outsourced processes in the food chain:

- Cold storage or freezing of ingredients or end products
- Transportation of food or ingredients
- Irradiation of ingredients or other materials
- Packaging
- Washing of tanks, transportation equipment, or facilities
- Grinding or mixing or weighing of ingredients

Additionally, this will also be linked to clause 7.3.5.1 of the standard given that the flow diagrams of these outsourced processes form part of the preliminary steps to enable hazard analysis.

Documentation Requirements (4.2)

In any type of organization, the incorporation of documents should be a task that adds value rather than one that reduces productivity by forming a heavy bureaucratic system. It is often argued that time is wasted by preparing such documentation, but the benefits are undeniable in the long term for organizations that create an efficient documentation system. Often, companies invest a lot of time in building an "HACCP Manual" when, in fact, it is used only as a showpiece to clients and auditors.

However, it is important to accurately document an FSMS. The use of documents is one of the easiest and direct ways to demonstrate to interested parties the capability of any organization to control food safety hazards.

Minimal documentation of an FSMS includes the following:

- The policy of food safety and its objectives
- Those documents required by the standard (including records)
- Those documents that the organization considers necessary

The third bullet includes requirements of client documentation, legal requirements, and organizational decisions to document a specified activity. Although the standard establishes a list of mandatory documents and records, it is rare to find a management system that has minimal documentation. The extension of documentation in a system depends on several factors. The following is an adaptation of a note from the ISO-9001:2008 standard.

The extent of the management system documentation can differ from one organization to another due to multiple factors, including

- the size of an organization and type of activities,
- the complexity of processes and their interactions, and
- the competence of personnel.

An organization must identify the legal requirements not only for local customers but for any country to which they intend to export their products. The following websites provide information about legal requirements in several countries as well as recommended codes of practice:

International Portal on Food Safety, Animal & Plant Health
`www.ipfsaph.org`

US Food and Drug Administration www.fda.gov
USDA Food Safety and Inspection Service www.fsis.usda.gov
Agriculture and Agri-food (Canada) www.agr.gc.ca
Codex Alimentarius Commission www.codexalimentarius.
net

*Category B Farming 2 (plants). Lettuce field in
Baja California, Mexico. Photo by the author.*

Addressing Requirements

ISO-22000:2005 does not require a document equivalent to the
quality manual, but for companies looking to implement these
requirements, it is best to design a food safety manual to address
the requirements of the standard (the "what") and the organization system (the "how"). Oftentimes, deficiencies in management
systems occur when the organization merely copies and pastes

fragments of the standard into its own documentation without defining how these requirements will be met.

For those organizations that decided to implement ISO-22000:2005 and already have a management system based on ISO-9001:2008, the best and easiest thing to do is to use the quality manual to include those requirements of ISO-22000:2005 in the organization's management system through cross-references (Annex A of ISO-22000:2005). The advantage is that both standards have requirements in common, which makes the process a lot easier. It is common to see food companies with ISO-9001:2008 and no HACCP implementing ISO-22000:2005 faster and easier than companies who have HACCP but do not have ISO-9001:2008.

When integrating ISO-22000:2005 into a management system, in addition to using the cross-references, the organization should use a document called PAS-99:2006 (Specification of Common Management System Requirements as a Framework for Integration). Figure 7 is built from this document and highlights the common elements.

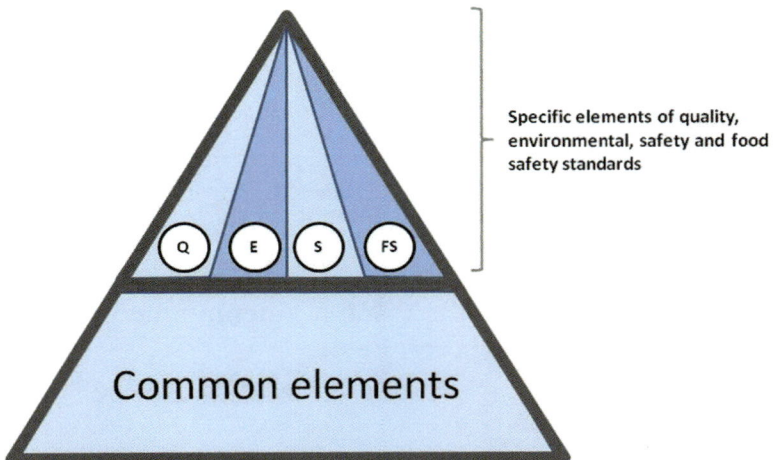

Figure 7 – Representation of an integrated management system (adapted from PAS-99:2006).

ISO-22000:2005 does not have exclusions (as does ISO-9001:2008). Therefore, when utilizing ISO-22000:2005, all the requirements must be applied. This does not mean that all requirements must be implemented. There are cases, for example, in which an organization did not implement any OPRP; this would be acceptable only if, as a result of its categorization of control measures (7.4.4), the organization determined that no control measure classified as an OPRP; hence, the requirement was applied but not implemented. Something similar will happen with the outsourced processes (4.1).

Clause 4.2.2 is about document control and is the same as 4.2.3 of ISO-9001:2008. This is an advantage to organizations that already have ISO-9001:2008 implemented since they will not have to take further action; the same applies to record control (4.2.3).

This clause also addresses the first documented procedure. This document defines protocols for inclusions, updates, and changes in documents, which require approval prior to execution so that the changes made in the documents can be identified. Precautions are implemented to avoid the unintended use of obsolete documents, the control of external documents (local, national, and international standards; standard methods of analysis; implementation guides; and so on), and methods to ensure its legibility and its availability in its points of use.

Procedure[8]	*Specified way to carry out an activity or a process.*

ISO-9000:2005 refers to the value of documentation in a management system in the quotation below:

Documentation enables communication of intent and consistency of action. Its use contributes to

- *achievement of conformity to customer requirements and quality improvement,*
- *provision of appropriate training,*

- *repeatability and traceability,*
- *provision of objective evidence, and*
- *evaluation of the effectiveness and continuing suitability of the quality management system.*

The standard establishes the following documents as minimally mandatory:

Documented Procedures

- Control of documents (4.2.2)
- Control of records (4.2.3)
- Corrections (7.10.1)
- Corrective action (7.10.2)
- Withdrawals (7.10.4)
- Internal audits (8.4.1)

Other required documents include the following:

- Outsourced processes (4.1)
- Food safety policy and objectives (5.2)
- Preliminary steps to enable hazard analysis (7.3.1)
- Raw materials, ingredients, and product-contact material descriptions (7.3.3.1)
- Characteristics of end products (7.3.3.2)
- Intended use (7.3.4)
- Flow diagrams (7.3.5.1) (refer to 7.3.1)
- Description of process steps and control measures (7.3.5.2) (in reference to 7.3.1)
- Selection and assessment of control measures (7.4.4)
- OPRP (7.5)
- HACCP plan (7.6)
- Determination of critical limits (7.6.3) (link to 8.2)
- Handling of potentially unsafe products (7.10.3.1)
- PRP (7.2) (note that the word "should" is used)
- Verification plan (7.8) (note: "in a form suitable for the organization's method of operation")

- Hazard assessment (7.4.3) (note: "the methodology used shall be described")
- Monitoring procedures (7.6.4) (note: relevant procedures)

Records are one of the most important elements in any management system as they provide evidence of compliance. A list of mandatory records is included at the end of this section, which might be useful during an implementation or audit. Beyond the requirements, it is important to consider any other activities that should also be recorded.

The following criteria are commonly used to decipher the length of time records ought to be kept:

- Shelf life
- Legal and client requirements
- For a defined period that enables traceability system assessment

Minimally required records include the following:

- External communication (5.6.1)
- Management review (5.8)
- Agreements or contracts defining responsibility and authority of external experts (6.2.1)
- Training records (6.2.2.)
- Verification and modifications of the PRP (7.2.3)
- Preliminary steps to enable hazard analysis (7.3.1)
- Records that demonstrate knowledge and experience of the food safety team (7.3.2)
- On-site flowcharts verification (7.3.5.1)
- Hazard identification (7.4.2.1)
- Determination of acceptable levels in the end product (7.4.2.3)
- Assessment of hazards results (7.4.3)
- Evaluation of control measures (7.4.4)
- OPRP monitoring (7.5)
- CCP monitoring (7.6)

- Verification results (7.8)
- Traceability records (7.9)
- Correction records (7.10.1)
- Evaluation of products manufactured under conditions where OPRP have not been conformed (7.10.1)
- Corrective actions (7.10.2)
- Cause, extent, and result of a withdrawal (7.10.4)
- Calibration results (8.3)
- Basis used for calibration or verification when it is not possible to use a traceable standard (8.3)
- Assessment and resulting actions when a measuring device is found not to conform to requirements (8.3)
- Internal audits (8.4.1)
- Result of the analysis of verification and resulting activities (8.4.3)
- System updating activities (8.5.2)

The documents and records required by the standard are certainly minimal, but it is rare to find a food safety management system where such minimal documentation is sufficient to keep a system running adequately.

Category C Processing 1 (perishable animal products). Fish processing in the Bến Tre Province, Vietnam. Photo by Carlos Jaimes.

5. – Management Responsibility

Management Commitment (5.1)

> *Top management shall provide evidence of its commitment to the development and implementation of the Food Safety Management System.*

TopManagement[8]	*Person or group of people who directs and controls an organization at the highest level.*

It is easy to see why it is important for top management be committed to the management system. The question remains: How is that evidence provided? Yet, this is never directly asked in an audit. Looking at it from an auditor's point of view, committed leadership is seen through proper planning for the implementation of the system, how the top management closely supervises the performance of the organization regarding food safety and plays an important role in communication activities both external and internal.

Symptoms of a noncommitted management are easy to spot and include the following:

- Delayed corrective actions without justification
- Unattended customer complaints
- Unattended audit findings
- No supervision over decisions taken into management review

When a third-party assessor finds these or similar situations, he or she can easily document a nonconformity against this requirement.

Food Safety Policy and Objectives (5.2)

Food Safety Policy[2]	Overall intentions and direction of an organization related to food safety as formally expressed by top management.

The requirements of the standard regarding the food safety policy are the following:

(a) Is appropriate to the role of the organization in the food chain
(b) Conforms with both statutory and regulatory requirements and with mutually agreed food safety requirements of customers
(c) Is communicated, implemented and maintained at all levels of the organization
(d) Is reviewed for continual suitability (see 5.8)
(e) Adequately addresses communication (see 5.6)
(f) Is supported by measurable objectives

The most common mistake in applying this requirement is disregarding the importance of communication, which is essential for any organization within the food chain.

No management system is complete without objectives. The ISO/TS 22004:2005 guide establishes that the food safety objectives should be *specific, measurable, achievable, relevant, and time-framed.* Food safety objectives are the basis for improving the food safety management system.

Category D Processing 2 (perishable and preserved vegetable products). Aseptic mango juice in Sinaloa, Mexico. Photo by Cesar Ramirez.

Food Safety Team Leader (5.5)

The responsibility and authority of the food safety leader is well-defined in the standard.

(a) *To manage the food safety team (see 7.3.2) and organize its work*
(b) *To ensure relevant training and education of the food safety team members (see 6.2.1)*
(c) *To ensure that the food safety management system is established, implemented, maintained and updated*
(d) *To report to the organization's top management on the effectiveness and suitability of the food safety management system*

Because the methodology for the hazard analysis requires teamwork, it is important when selecting a leader to take into consideration that most of the planning and verification work will be done as a team. Thus, the leader's authority must be clearly communicated (see 5.4).

Communication (5.6)

Communication, without a doubt, is one of the most relevant aspects in this standard; no organization within the food chain can be isolated and ensure safe products.

FoodChain[2]	*Sequence of the stages and operations involved in the production, processing, distribution, storage, and handling of a food and its ingredients, from primary production to consumption. Note 1: This includes the production of feed for food-producing animals and for animals intended for food production. Note 2: The food chain also includes the production of materials intended to come into contact with food or raw materials.*

To understand the importance of interactive communication, it would be relevant to mention that the clause referring to communication in ISO-9001:2008 is fourteen times less extensive than in ISO-22000:2005. This section deals with both external communication (with clients, customers, suppliers, government officials, etc.) and internal communication, largely due to changes in the organization. In the interrelationships diagram, it is easy to observe that communication directly impacts several aspects of the FSMS requirements such as the food safety policy, management system update, input information for management review, competition, evaluation of verification results, and continuous improvement. In other words, communication is to ISO-22000:2005 what continuous improvement is to ISO-9001:2008.

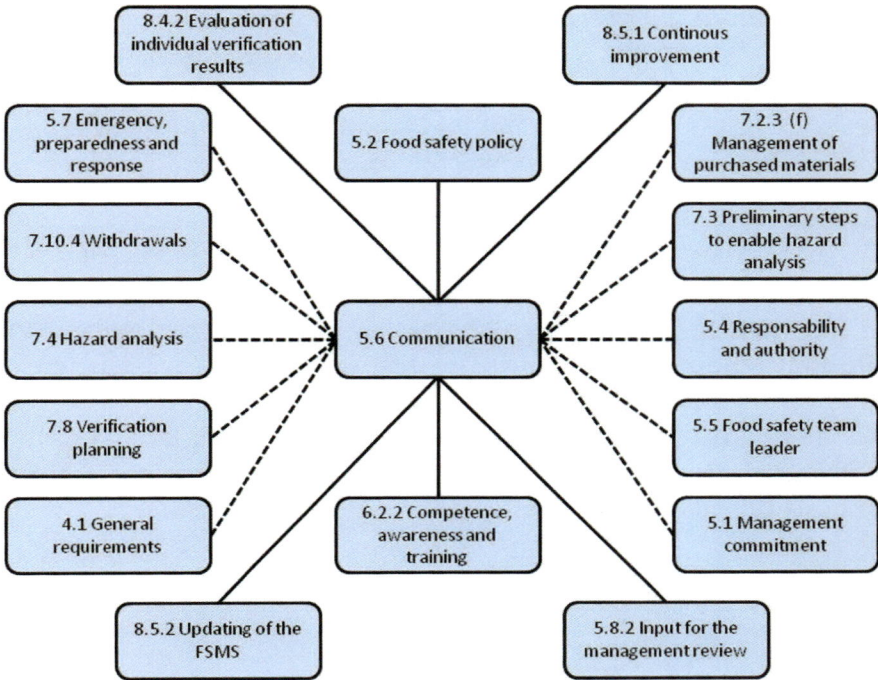

Figure 8 – Interrelationship diagram. Communication-related clauses.

Emergency Preparedness and Response (5.7)

It is incredible how this succinct requirement needs a considerable amount of work for its implementation. In order to put this into context within the standard ISO-22000:2005, it is helpful to keep the following statement in mind:

You don't only need to design a system to prevent food safety hazards, but also that system must include planning on what to do in case of emergency situations.

ISO/TS-22004:2005 mentions some potential emergency situations that can impact food safety. They are *fire, flooding, bioterrorism and sabotage, energy failure, vehicle accidents, and contamination of the environment.*

15

Contingency Planning[12]	Consideration of the potentially serious incidents that could affect the operations of the organization and the formulation of a plan(s) to prevent or mitigate the effects and to enable the organization to operate as normally as possible.

Generally, there are two principles to fulfill this requirement.

The first principle involves an organization's determining potential emergency situations within its line of work and creating specific action plans for each identified emergency situation. This mechanism includes a periodic review of the plans as well as criteria for determining additional emergency situations that were not considered at the outset.

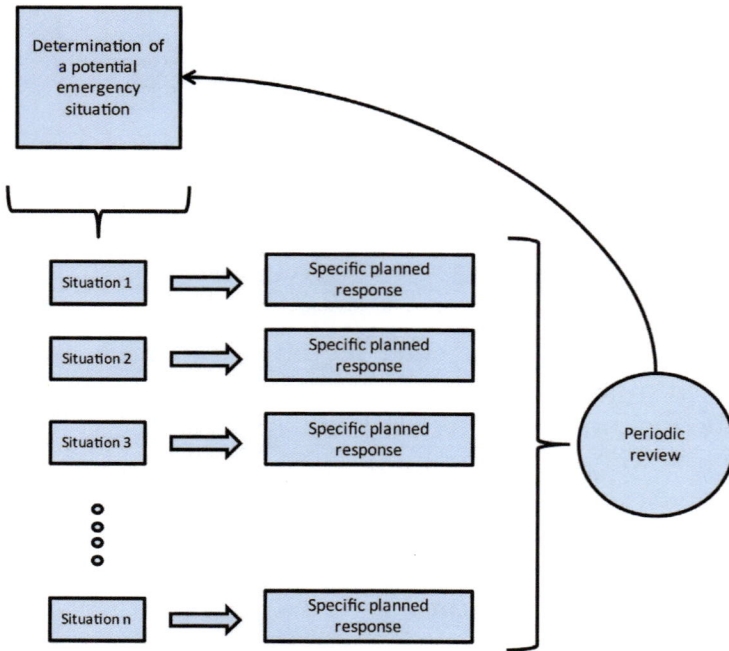

Figure 9 – Emergency preparedness and response. Conventional model.

Alternatively, an organization can determine "triggers" of potential emergencies using staff members who are designated and trained by the organization to detect a potential incident. These persons are trained in how to react and communicate to certain people or groups within the organization by a previously designed mechanism. Decisions and actions can then be made once the situation is dimensioned by a standardized method. This is better explained using figure 10.

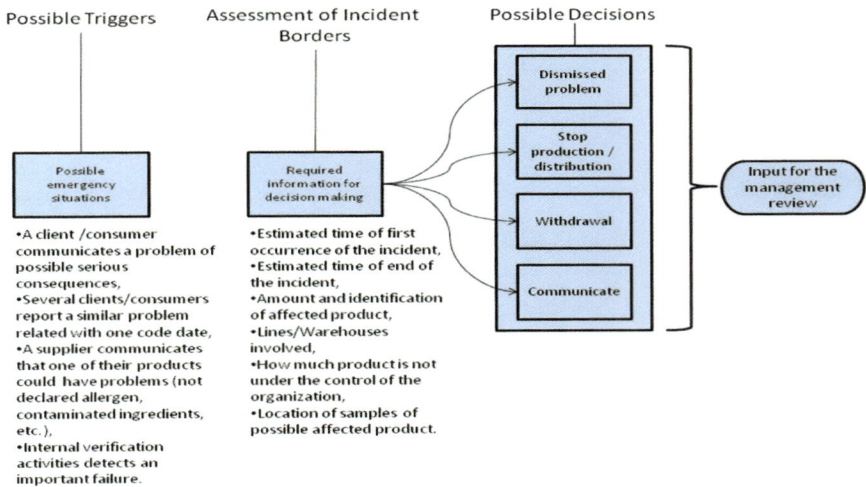

Figure 10 – Emergency preparedness and response. Generic plan.

In the next interrelationship diagram (figure 11), notice that clause 5.7 (Emergency preparedness and response) is directly linked to only one clause; the other six, however, are shown to have inherently significant relationships.

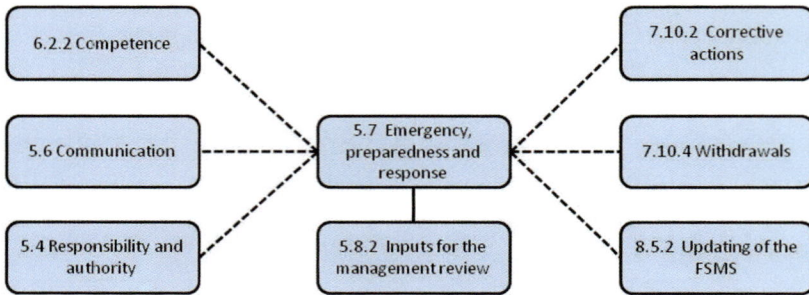

Figure 11 – Interrelationship diagram. Emergency preparedness and response-related clauses.

Management Review (5.8)

Management review is related to the "act" part of the PDCA cycle.

Top management shall review the organization's Food Safety Management System at planned intervals to ensure its continuing suitability, adequacy and effectiveness.	
Effectiveness [8]	*Extent to which planned activities are realized and planned results achieved.*

This review is performed using the process approach (figure 12).

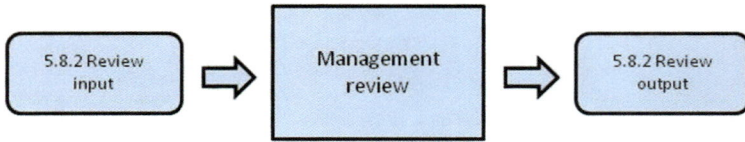

Figure 12 – Interrelationship diagram. Management review.

The input is described in section 5.8.2, but other relevant information can also be added. Take the points mentioned in 5.8.2 as a meeting agenda.

A common mistake is to regard this meeting as one for information only, without starting (and recording) decisions and actions arising from that point. The results of the management review should include evidence of actions and decisions related to the

assurance of food safety (4.1),
improvement of the effectiveness of the Food Safety Management System (8.5),
resource needs (6.1), and
revisions of the organization's food safety policy and related objectives (5.2).

The frequency of management reviews depends on each organization. Some aspects of reviews are done more frequently, whereas others occur less frequently; this is completely acceptable, depending on the needs of each organization.

Category E Processing 3 (products with long shelf life).
Frozen donut line in Nuevo Leon, Mexico. Photo by Erika Cortez.

6. – Management of Resources

The organization shall provide adequate resources for the establishment, implementation, maintenance and updating of the Food Safety Management System.

Human Resources (6.2)

ISO-22000:2005 is clear in its requirements for the use of consultants to help the organization maintain its FSMS. Any organization choosing to hire a consultant for the implementation and maintenance of the management system must have a contract where the responsibility and authority of this consultant is established officially.

The factors for choosing a consultant will always depend on each organization's needs. If an organization already has a management system implemented like ISO-9001:2008, it is essential to hire a consultant who has the capacity to integrate the requirements of ISO-22000:2005 to the current management system, and not try to implement a parallel system. The best way to verify the competence of an FSMS consultant is to request his or her certification as consultant/auditor. The most reputable certification programs are the International Register of Certified Auditors (IRCA) at `www.irca.org` and RABQSA International, Inc. at www.rabqsa.com. Both pages provide a complete directory of certified people. Keep in mind that some food safety consultants are unfamiliar with management systems, so make sure the consultant you hire does not fall in this category.

| **Competence**[8] | *Demonstrated ability to apply knowledge and skill.* |

Adapting from the guide for audit "ISO-9001 Auditing Practices Group Guidance On: Auditing Competence and the 'effectiveness of actions taken.'" An organization requires the following to comply with clause 6.2.2.

- Identify what competencies staff require to perform tasks that affect food safety
- Determine whether staff already performing these tasks possess the required competencies
- Decide what additional competencies are required
- Decide how to obtain these additional competencies (e.g., staff training [internal or external]; practical and theoretical training; hiring of new, competent staff; and assigning existing, competent staff different tasks)
- Train, hire, or reassign staff
- Review efficiency of actions taken to satisfy competence needs
- Periodically review staff competency

The requirement also mentions the following:

The organization shall (c) ensure that personnel responsible for monitoring corrections and corrective actions of the Food Safety Management System are trained.

Monitoring responsibility is primarily linked to requirements 7.5 (OPRP) and 7.6 (HACCP plan). It is important to ensure that training records and training materials are kept on those responsible for monitoring activities in the operational prerequisite programmes and critical control points. The responsibility of corrections and corrective actions is also linked to section 7.10 (Control of nonconformities).

Infrastructure (6.3) and Work Environment (6.4)

These clauses are closely related to the prerequisite programmes (7.2) (figure 13).

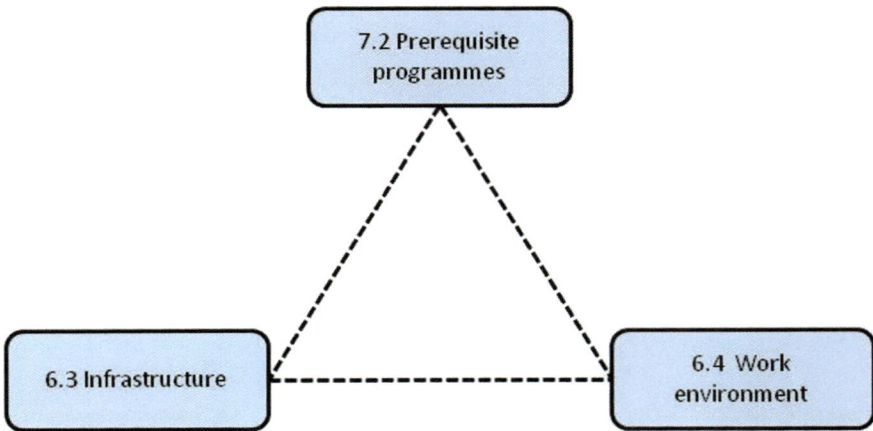

Figure 13 – Interrelationship diagram.
Work environment conditions for product realization.

Infrastructure[8]	*System of facilities, equipment, and services needed for the operation of an organization.*
Work environment[8]	*Set of conditions under which work is performed.*

For this reason, infrastructure and work environment are considered within the explanation of the prerequisite programmes.

Category F (feed). Fermentation process for feed production in Zhejiang, China. Photo by Henry Turlington.

7. – Planning and Realization of Safe Products

The organization shall implement, operate and ensure the effectiveness of the planned activities and any changes to those activities. This includes PRP(s) as well as operational PRP(s) and/or the HACCP plan.

Part seven of the standard—by far the longest—is where the commonly known twelve steps of HACCP are found, as well as the control of nonconformities.

HACCP[1]	A system which identifies, evaluates, and controls hazards which are significant for food safety.

The introduction states that the methodology of the Codex was adopted for the elaboration of this standard. The Codex describes the twelve steps for the implementation of HACCP as follows:

1. Assemble HACCP team.
2. Describe product.
3. Identify intended use.
4. Construct flow diagram.

5. On-site confirmation of the flow diagram.
6. List all potential hazards associated with each step, conduct a hazard analysis, and consider any measures to control identified hazards.
7. Determine critical control points.
8. Establish critical limits for each CCP.
9. Establish a monitoring system for each CCP.
10. Establish corrective actions.
11. Establish verification procedures.
12. Establish documentation and record keeping.

The main differences between the Codex and ISO-22000:2005 are illustrated in figure 14, which includes a modification from the original in ISO/TS-22004:2005, locating the validation of the control measures prior to the categorization.

Category G (catering). Catering services in Coahuila, Mexico.
Photo by Juan R. Cardenas.

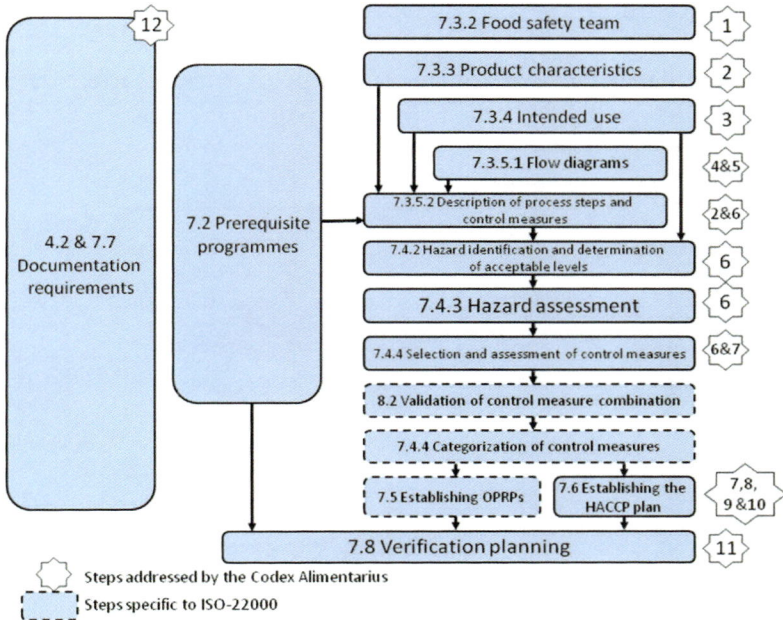

Figure 14 – Food safety planning (adapted from ISO/TS-22004:2005).

The most important differences are the validation of food safety control measures (8.2), which will be discussed in the next section, as well as the operational prerequisite programmes (7.5). However, two more relevant differences exist:

- The Codex Alimentarius is a recommended code of practice and not an auditable standard as is ISO-22000:2005.
- The Codex Alimentarius describes only the planning phase for the production of safe products. Keep in mind ISO-22000:2005 also covers the other three phases of any management system (do, check, and act).

The main adaptation in figure 14 is the repetition of the clause 7.4.4 in a dotted box to elucidate the guidance provided in ISO/TS-22004:2005 that mentions that the effects of the combination of control measures are validated prior to categorization.

This statement also corresponds with figures 1 and 3 in that specification (figures 2 and 19 in this book).

Until not too long ago, the concept of control measures in the traditional HACCP was described as follows:

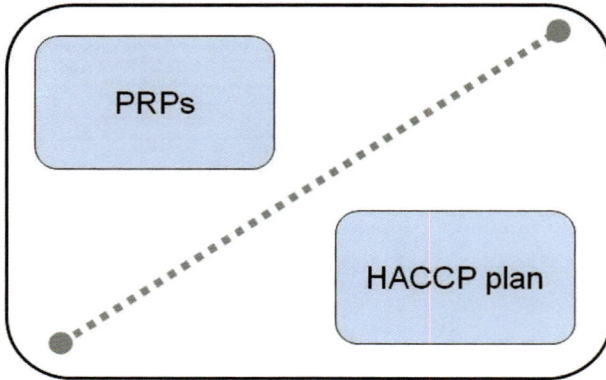

Figure 15 – Control measures. Traditional HACCP.

In ISO-22000:2005, this is developed and modified to include OPRP(s), as shown below in figure 16:

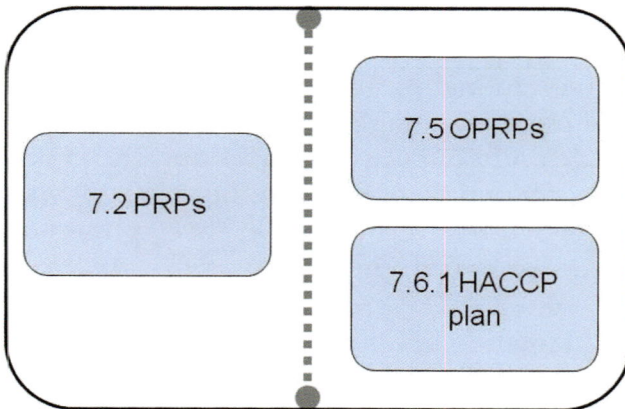

Figure 16 – Control measures. ISO-22000:2005.

Unlike ISO-22000:2005, the Codex suggests focusing control at the CCPs.

The intent of the HACCP system is to focus control at Critical Control Points (CCPs). Redesign of the operation should be considered if a hazard which must be controlled is identified but no CCPs are found.

In ISO-22000:2005, three types of control measures stand out.

PRP Prerequisite Programme[2]	*<Food Safety> basic conditions and activities that are necessary to maintain a hygienic environment throughout the food chain suitable for the production, handling and provision of safe end products and safe food for human consumption.*
Operational PRP Operational Prerequisite Programme[2]	*PRP Identified by hazard analysis as essential in order to control the likelihood of introducing food safety hazard to and/or the contamination or proliferation of food safety hazards in the product(s) or in the processing environment.*
CCP Critical ControlPoint[2]	*<Food Safety> step at which control can be applied and is essential to prevent or eliminate a food safety hazard or reduce it to an acceptable level.*

Occasionally, the definitions alone do not identify the differences or scope of these terms. These terms will be clarified once hazard analysis is examined later in this section.

Prerequisite Programmes (7.2)

In the Codex, the following can be read:

Prior to application of HACCP to any sector of the food chain, that sector should have in place prerequisite programs such as good hygienic practices according to the Codex General Principles of Food Hygiene, the appropriate Codex Codes of Practice, and appropriate food safety requirements. These prerequisite programs to HACCP, including training, should be well established, fully operational and verified in order to facilitate the successful application and implementation of the HACCP system.

The necessary PRP(s) will depend on the segment of the food chain where the organization is located. Some examples of these PRP(s) are the following:

- Good Agricultural Practices (GAP)
- Good Veterinarian Practices (GVP)
- Good Manufacturing Practices (GMP)
- Good Distribution Practices (GDP)

In Annex C of the ISO-22000:2005 standard, a list of the Recommended Code of Practices published by the Commission of Codex is provided. These can be obtained at `www.codexalimentarius.net`.

Although the prerequisite programmes have been discussed and applied for years, neither the Codex nor ISO-15161:2001 (guidelines on the application of ISO-9001 for the food and drink industry) provides a definition. As mentioned earlier, these programmes help to maintain basic hygienic conditions, but how can it be established which are the right ones? Each organization will make that determination. ISO-22000:2005 is a management standard; therefore, as a generic document, it cannot establish specifications or levels of execution. That is why the food safety team will determine and approve what those conditions and basic activities will be to maintain an adequate hygienic environment. For this, the food safety team will have to consider the following:

When selecting and/or establishing PRP(s), the organization shall consider and utilize appropriate information [e.g. statutory and regulatory requirements, customer requirements, recognized guidelines, Codex Alimentarius Commission (Codex) principles and codes of practices, national, international or sector standards].

By the end of 2008, a specification called PAS-220:2008 (now called ISO/TS-22002-1:2009) was published. This document established the prerequisite programmes that must be implemented in food manufacturing organizations whose main clients are retailers. PAS-220:2008 takes section 7.2.3 of ISO-22000:2005 as an index and provides specifications for PRP(s) in food manufacturing companies. The requirements in this document can only be implemented together and never separated from ISO-22000:2005.

Companies that have completed the implementation of ISO-22000:2005 together with ISO/TS-22002:2009 can obtain a certification called FSSC-22000:2010 (Food Safety System Certification), which is now accepted by the Global Food Safety Initiative (GFSI). For more information, visit **www.fssc22000.com**.

Category H (retail outlets, shops, wholesalers). Vegetable shelves in Baja California, Mexico. Photo by the author.

Preliminary Steps To Enable Hazard Analysis (7.3)

It was previously mentioned that the hazard analysis and all its methodology must be outlined primarily as a team. This is the reason the formation of a multidisciplinary team is so relevant; such teams must have enough experience and knowledge of the products and processes.

It is not always easy to work as a team; it is especially difficult when the designated food safety team leader does not possess the qualifications to hold such a position. The size of the team will always depend on the size of the organization. Try to keep it compact and functional.

A food safety team may generally be formed of staff of one or more of the following departments:

- Production/Manufacturing
- Quality Assurance
- Research and Development
- Engineering/Maintenance
- Human Resources
- Warehousing

Appointing a team within an organization is always easy, whereas making this team work adequately is always a challenge.

Clauses 7.3.3.1, 7.3.3.2, and 7.3.5.2 establish that raw materials, ingredients, materials in contact with products, final products, and processes will be described in documents. In some cases, such descriptions were already documented in specifications of ingredients or final products or in process descriptions and work instructions—in which case, it is necessary to review only if such documents comply with what is required in the clauses previously mentioned.

Specification [8]	*Document stating requirements.*

End Product[2]	Product that will undergo no further processing or transformation by the organization. A product that undergoes further processing or transformation by another organization is an end product in the context of the first organization and a raw material or an ingredient in the context of the second organization.

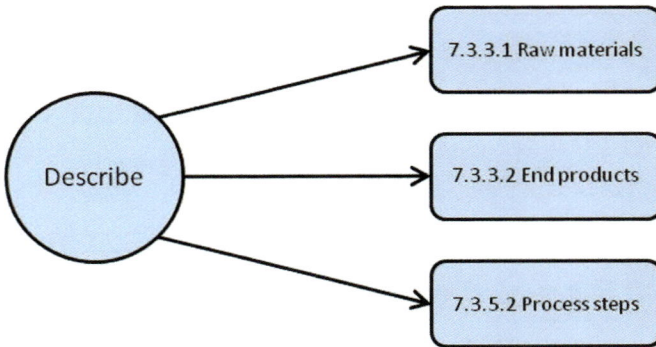

Figure 17 – Description of relevant elements to enable hazard analysis.

The purpose of composing these descriptions is mainly to facilitate hazard identification.

Food Safety[2]	Concept that food will not cause harm to the consumer when it is prepared and/or eaten according to its intended use.

It is useless to apply the necessary required precautions if a possibility exists that the intended use will not be respected. The intended use will be described in documents and will include

- reasonable manipulation expected from the final product,
- inappropriate, unintentional manipulation,

as well as

- user groups,
- consumer groups (when appropriate), and
- consumer groups especially vulnerable to specific hazards

Flow Diagram [2]	*Schematic and systematic presentation of the sequence and interactions of steps.*

In the preparation of flow diagrams, it is essential that all components included are easily understood.

Flow diagrams shall be clear, accurate and sufficiently detailed.

A flow chart without sufficient details would make hazard identification difficult.

The standard also mentions that flow diagrams should include the following:

(a) The sequence and interaction of all steps in the operation
(b) Any outsourced processes and subcontracted work
(c) Where raw materials, ingredients and intermediate products enter the flow
(d) Where reworking and recycling take place
(e) Where end products, intermediate products, by-products and waste are released or removed.

It is very useful that some rules of representation are established before the preparation of the flow diagrams and should be the basis for the onsite confirmation of the flow diagrams from the food safety team.

Figure 18 shows the relationships of the related clauses with the preliminary steps to enable the hazard analysis.

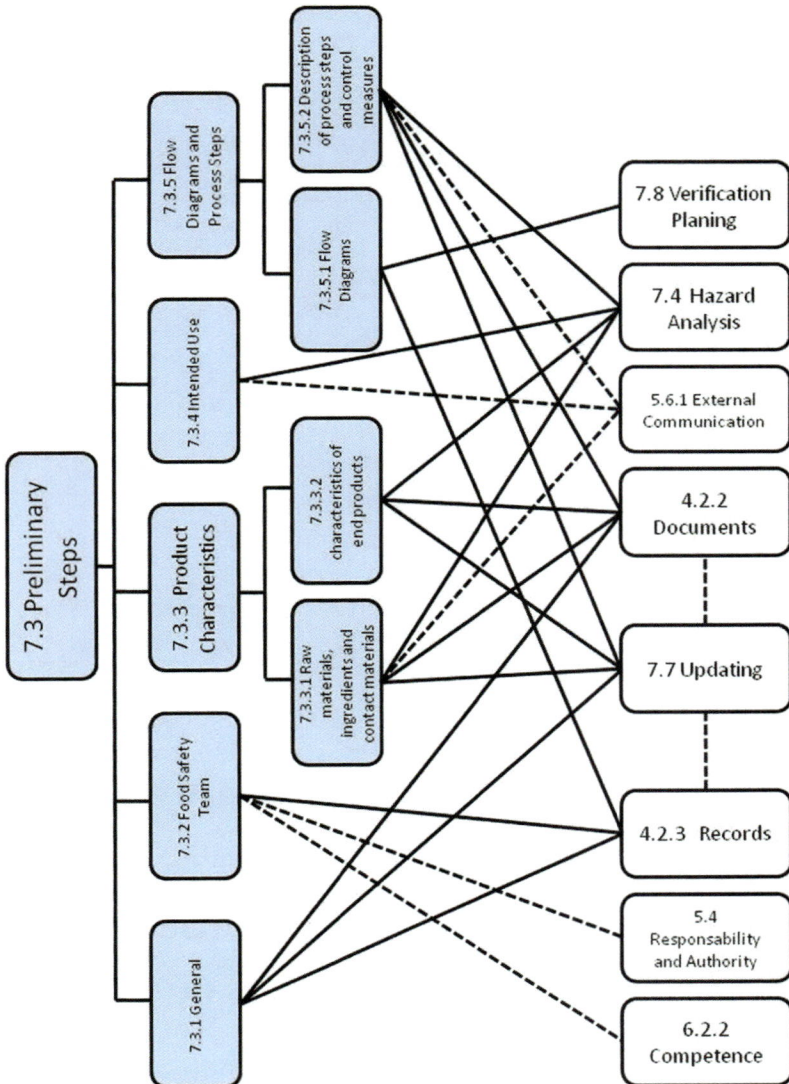

Figure 18 – Interrelationship diagram. Preliminary steps to enable hazard analysis.

Category I (services). Installation and start-up of a specialty packaging line for a Canadian pork processor. Photo courtesy of Charlottetown Metal Products.

Hazard Analysis (7.4)

The food safety team shall conduct a hazard analysis to determine which hazards need to be controlled, the degree of control required to ensure food safety, and which combination of control measures is required.

FoodSafety Hazard[2]	*Biological, chemical or physical agent in food, or condition of food, with the potential to cause an adverse health effect. Note: The term "hazard" is not to be confused with the term "risk" which, in the context of food safety, means a function of the probability of and adverse health effect (e.g. becoming diseased) and the severity of that effect (death, hospitalization, absence from work, etc.) when exposed to a specified hazard. Risk is defined in ISO/IEC Guide 51 as the combination of the probability of occurrence of harm and the severity of that harm.*

Hazard analysis in ISO-22000:2005 consists basically of three parts:

- Hazard identification and acceptable level determination
- Hazard evaluation
- Selection and classification of control measures

The food safety team will identify all predictable, reasonable hazards, taking into consideration all aspects mentioned in 7.4.2.1.

(a) *The preliminary information and data collected according to 7.3*
(b) *Experience*
(c) *External information including, to the extent possible, epidemiological and other historical data*
(d) *Information from the food chain on food safety hazards that may be of relevance for the safety of the end products, intermediate products and the food at consumption*

The acceptable level of the hazard in the final product should be determined. While there is no official definition for "acceptable level of the hazard," ISO/TS-22004:2005 clarifies it the following way:

Acceptablelevel of the hazard[5]	*The level of a particular hazard in the end product of the organization that is needed at the next step in the food chain to ensure food safety.*

The term "acceptable level of the hazard" often gets confused with "critical limit" of a CCP. The first is commonly linked with legal and/or statutory requirements, client requirements, and intended use. The second one is generally related to process parameters and is commonly the result of a validation.

Once hazards are identified, they must be evaluated. In clause 7.4.3, two evaluations are mentioned. Therefore, it is important to carry out the mentioned evaluation in the second paragraph, and then follow it with the evaluation in the first paragraph.

> *Each food safety hazard shall be evaluated according to the possible severity of adverse health effects and the likelihood of their occurrence. The methodology used shall be described, and the results of the food safety hazard assessment shall be recorded.*

The food safety team should define the methodology prior to using it in the evaluation; this way, the risk will be evaluated. It is important to highlight the second note of section 3.3 of ISO-22000:2005.

The best way to define a method is to determine levels of likelihood of occurrence and adverse health effect levels and then propose a description for each one. It is really important to keep this method simple and direct. The following (tables 1 and 2) can be used as examples.

Likelihood level	Description
High	An inherent/intrinsic food safety hazard for a particular raw material, process step, or a particular work environment.
Medium	Food safety hazard that can be associated with a particular raw material, process step, or work environment and could be present in a moderate frequency.
Low	Food safety hazard not usually associated with a particular raw material, process step, or work environment.

Table 1 – Example of classification of three levels of likelihood for food safety hazards to determine risks.

Adverse health effect level	Description
High	Any hazard that results in a life-threatening effect (immediate or long term), especially for vulnerable consumers (babies, the elderly, and persons with an immunosuppressed system).
Medium	Any hazard that results in a severe but not life-threatening effect (hospitalization, severe illness, or long absence from work/school)
Low	Any hazard that is neither life threatening nor a serious adverse health effect but may result in undesirable effects (discomfort, etc.)

Table 2 – Example of classification of three levels of adverse health effects caused by food safety hazards to determine risks.

The result is a measure of risks used later to define

- the monitoring frequency in control measures,
- the verification frequency,
- the rigorousness of the verification methods, and
- other important aspects for the FSMS.

After evaluating the hazards, it is necessary to appraise the factors mentioned in the first paragraph of 7.4.3. This is the decision tree for the hazard analysis published in ISO/TS-22004:2005. In this decision tree, the two sections of clause 7.4.3 are referred to as the following:

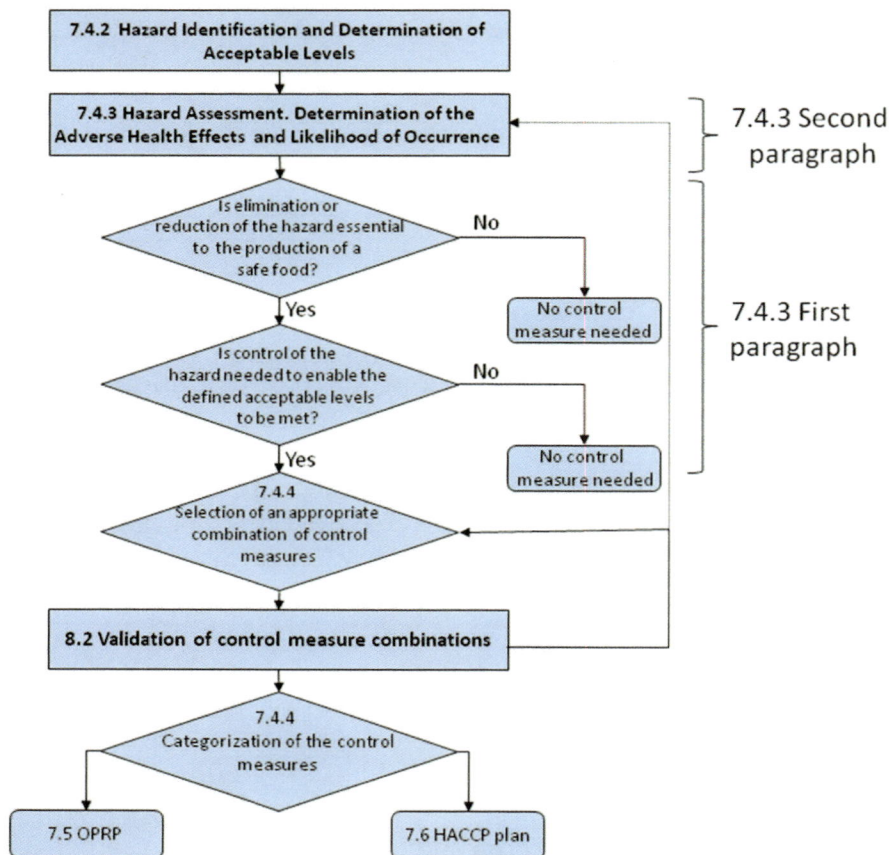

Figure 19 – Decision tree (from ISO/TS-22004:2005).

Take note of the following:

> *A hazard assessment shall be conducted to determine, for each food safety hazard identified (see 7.4.2), whether its elimination or reduction to acceptable levels is essential to the production of a safe food, and whether its control is needed to enable the defined acceptable levels to be met.*

Identified Hazards (Inputs)

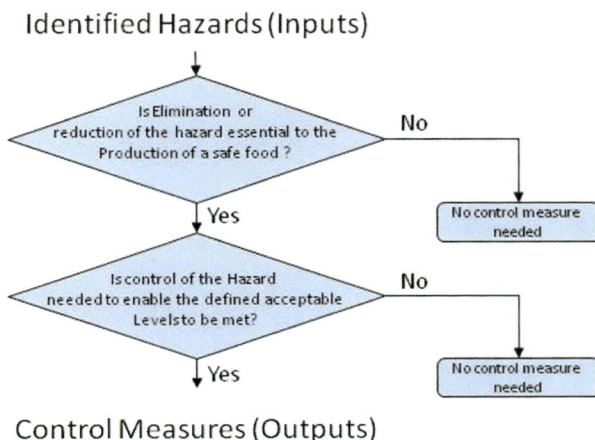

Control Measures (Outputs)

Figure 20 – Decision tree [section] (from ISO/TS-22004:2005).

The first paragraph of 7.4.3 refers to a specific section of the decision tree (figure 20).

Is the elimination or reduction of a hazard essential for the production of a safe food?
Possible negative answers to this question include the following:

- When an identified hazard in one of the ingredients does not have the probability of exceeding acceptable limits in the final product because it is at a very low level in some ingredient that is in very low proportion in the end product.
- When the hazard will be controlled in the next stage of the food chain.

Here is the second question:

Is hazard control necessary to achieve the acceptable levels?
Possible negative answers to this question include the following:

- When a control measure specific for eliminating/reducing the identified hazard is implemented in a previous stage of the food chain.

- When inherent conditions of the production process exceed by far the minimum to eliminate or reduce the identified hazard.

A document was published by the International Trade Center and ISO in 2008 called "An easy-to-use checklist for small business. Are you ready?" The ISO/TS-22004:2005 includes a decision tree and is formulated in the following way:

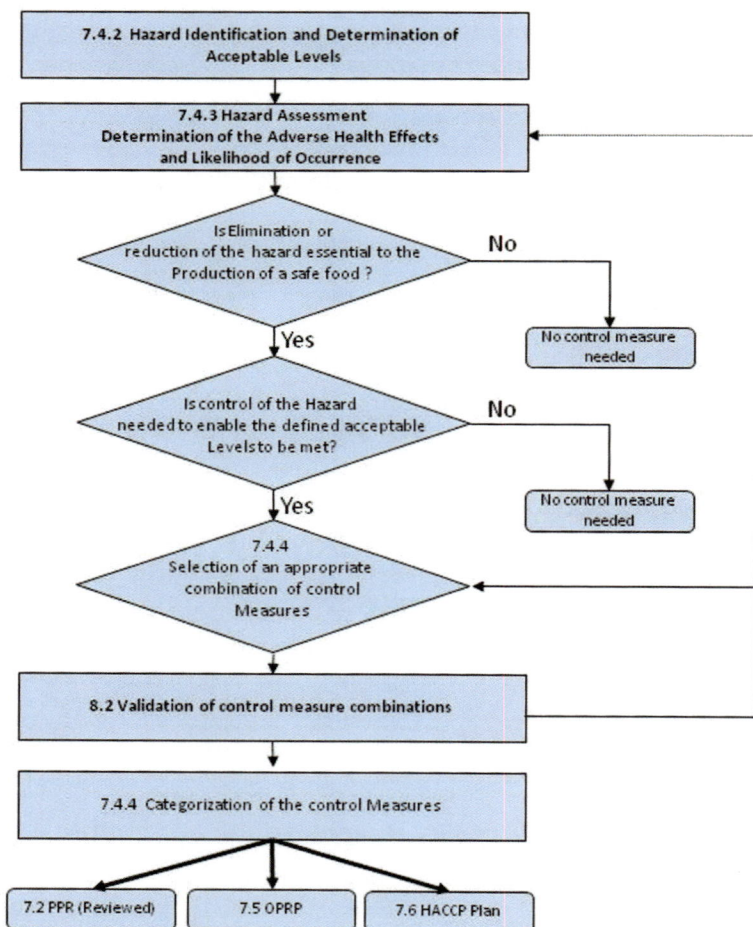

Figure 21 – Decision tree from ISO-22000 Food Safety Management System Guideline[18].

As illustrated, a possible classification of control measures would be a reviewed prerequisite programme, which is considered in the following orientation included in ISO/TS-22004:2005:

Where a control measure cannot be validated, it cannot be included within a HACCP plan or in OPRP(s), but it can be applied within PRP(s).

A control measure is not feasible for validation when it cannot be applied or when it is not practical for application in at least one of the criteria listed in the validation section. This subject will be explained in detail in section eight of this book.

To start this activity, it is important to keep in mind the position of the organization inside the food chain. Several food safety hazards can be identified, but controls might be necessary only in certain links of the food chain. For example, a common food safety hazard, *Staphylococcus aureus*, will surely be identified in the hazard analysis of primary producer's organizations (link 3 in figure 22) and also in a hazard analysis in a food manufacturer's organizations (link 4 in figure 22), but the controls will be different in both links of the food chain. Also, a food manufacturer (links 4 or 5 in figure 22) and an equipment manufacturer (link 11 in figure 22) could identify metal fragments (another common food safety hazard) from equipment as food safety hazards, but the controls will be very different.

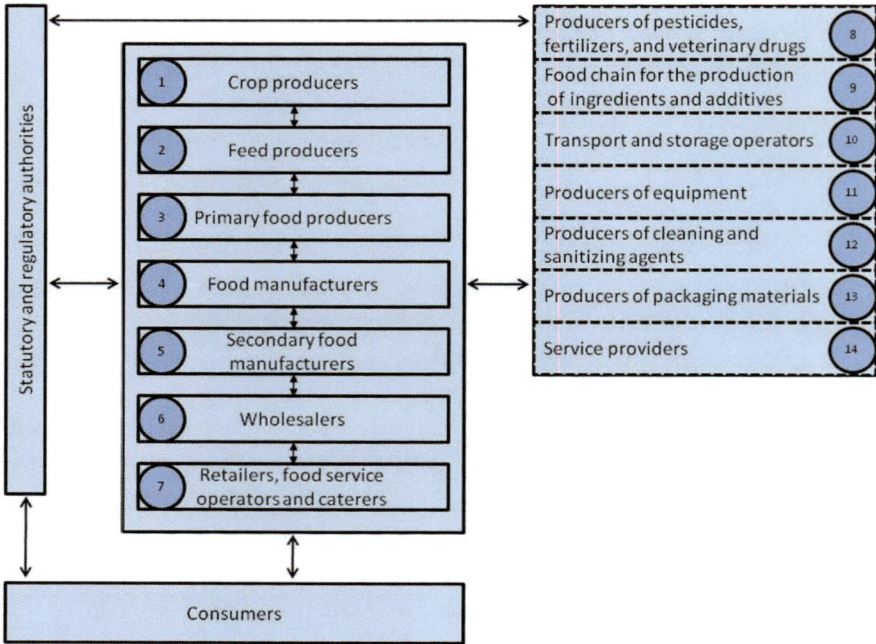

Figure 22 – Example of communication within the food chain (adapted from ISO-22000:2005).

Let us use the decision tree (figure 20) with some examples to explain requirement 7.2.3 (first paragraph) and requirement 7.4.4 (Selection of control measures). When the first question of the decision tree is answered "no" for the food safety team, the second does not require an answer. If either the first or the second question is answered no, a justification should be recorded. For each of the hazards where both questions were answered yes, a control measure will be selected. This must take into consideration all control measures described to comply with requirement 7.3.5.2.

These are only examples to provide a better explanation of the requirements, as the final responsibility in the hazard analysis is for the food safety team. For an organization that produces raw milk (link 3, see figure 22), the food safety hazard *Staphylococcus aureus* will be identified and could be evaluated as such:

Identified hazard	Is elimination or reduction of the hazard essential to the production of a safe food? (7.4.3)	Is control of the hazard needed to enable the defined acceptable levels to be met? (7.4.3)	Rationalization	Selected control measure (7.4.4)
Staphylococcus aureus in raw milk	Yes	No	Not in this link of the food chain. Raw milk will be pasteurized in the next step of the food chain.	N/A

Table 3 – Example of hazard evaluation and selection of control measure(s) for *Staphylococcus aureus* in primary production.

This could be the hazard analysis for a food manufacturer positioned in links four or five (figure 22) for the same food safety hazard in the same raw material.

Identified hazard	Is elimination or reduction of the hazard essential to the production of a safe food? (7.4.3)	Is control of the hazard needed to enable the defined acceptable levels to be met? (7.4.3)	Rationalization	Selected control measure (7.4.4)
Staphylococcus aureus in raw milk	Yes	Yes	N/A	Pasteurizer

Table 4 – Example of hazard evaluation and selection of control measure(s) for *Staphylococcus aureus* in a food manufacturing facility.

Another good example of an important food safety hazard that would be evaluated in a different way is glass fragments. A glass bottle manufacturer (link 13 in figure 22) could identify in its hazard analysis a series of defects in glass bottles that can create glass fragments that could harm consumers. Also, a food manufacturer that uses glass bottles as packaging material (link 4 or 5 in figure 22) should also identify glass fragments as food safety hazards. Contamination with glass fragments could occur when a bottle bursts inside the filler equipment, and the glass fragments enter uncovered bottles.

For a glass container manufacturer, the evaluation might read as follows:

Identified hazard	Is elimination or reduction of the hazard essential to the production of a safe food? (7.4.3)	Is control of the hazard needed to enable the defined acceptable levels to be met? (7.4.3)	Rationalization	Selected control measure (7.4.4)
Defects in bottles that can result in glass fragments inside the container (bird swing, chipped finish, choked neck, internal fused glass, etc.)	Yes	Yes	N/A	Electronic bottle inspector

Table 5 – Example of hazard evaluation and selection of control measure(s) for glass fragments in a glass container manufacturer.

A food manufacturer, such as a brewing company or a soft drink bottling company, would have an evaluation similar to this:

Identified hazard	Is elimination or reduction of the hazard essential to the production of a safe food? (7.4.3)	Is control of the hazard needed to enable the defined acceptable levels to be met? (7.4.3)	Rationalization	Selected control measure (7.4.4)
Glass fragments after a bottle bursts inside the filler	Yes	Yes	N/A	Glass breakage procedure

Table 6 – Example of hazard evaluation and selection of control measure(s) for glass fragments in a food manufacturer facility that uses glass as packaging material.

There can also be situations in which the same hazard analysis, a food safety hazard, will be identified in two processes/operations or ingredients, and the hazard can be evaluated in the same way. A confectionery manufacturer could identify metal fragments as a food safety hazard in raw materials and also in process equipment.

Identified hazard	Is elimination or reduction of the hazard essential to the production of a safe food? (7.4.3)	Is control of the hazard needed to enable the defined acceptable levels to be met? (7.4.3)	Rationalization	Selected control measure (7.4.4)
Metal fragments from ingredients (sugar)	Yes	Yes	N/A	Metal detector after the wrapper
Metal fragments from damaged equipment	Yes	Yes	N/A	Metal detector after the wrapper

Table 7 – Example of hazard evaluation and selection of control measure(s) for metal fragments identified in more than one raw material/process step in a confectionery manufacturer.

Some food safety hazards may not require elimination or reduction in certain links. A bakery that uses iodized salt as one of its ingredients could evaluate one chemical food safety hazard in this way:

Identified hazard	Is elimination or reduction of the hazard essential to the production of a safe food? (7.4.3)	Is control of the hazard needed to enable the defined acceptable levels to be met? (7.4.3)	Rationalization	Selected control measure (7.4.4)
Lead present in salt	No	—	No control measure is needed for this food safety hazard. The salt content in the finished product is too low to exceed acceptable levels in the end product. Salt comes from approved vendor.	N/A

Table 8 – Example of hazard evaluation and selection of control measure(s) for lead in a bakery plant.

In some situations, PRP(s) and additional control measures are simultaneously required. In the next example, a food manufacturer that receives raw milk for its products usually communicates regularly with primary producers of milk to ensure Good Veterinarian Practices are implemented as a PRP in order to control food safety hazards such as the presence of antibiotics in milk. It is a common practice, however, to implement a rapid test during reception as a second check.

Identified hazard	Is elimination or reduction of the hazard essential to the production of a safe food? (7.4.3)	Is control of the hazard needed to enable the defined acceptable levels to be met? (7.4.3)	Rationalization	Selected control measure (7.4.4)
Antibiotics in raw milk (amoxicillin, ampicillin, cephapirin, cloxacillin, penicillin, and others)	Yes	Yes	N/A	(1) Good Veterinarian Practices implemented with primary producers and (2) Antibiotic test during milk reception

Table 9 – Example of hazard evaluation and selection of control measure(s) for antibiotics in a dairy plant.

For the classification of control measures (second part of requirement 7.4.4), the following decision-making tree is proposed:

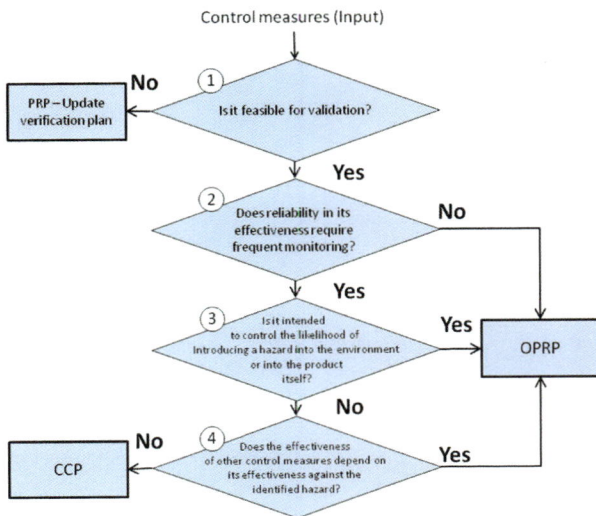

Figure 23 – Decision tree for the classification of control measures.

Control Measure[2]	<Food Safety> action or activity that can be used to prevent or eliminate a food safety hazard or reduce it to an acceptable level.

It is important to emphasize that the input of this decision tree is the output of the decision tree in figure 21. This decision tree is a simpler and more practical adaptation of the one proposed in one of the drafts of the standard (ISO-DIS-22000).

The most important difference between the decision tree published in ISO/TS-22004:2005 and the one in the Codex is that the input for the first one are the identified hazards, whereas the input for the second one are the process steps. This makes the ISO/TS-22004:2005 decision tree more practical and easier to utilize. Besides, the Codex decision tree does not have OPRP as a possible output, which is not allowed by ISO-22000:2005 since the methodology for the classification of control measures requires the OPRP as a possible result, even when the organization could not have identified one in the end.

At this time, it is appropriate to use some of the selected control measures from the previous examples to explain this requirement. Again, these examples are for didactic purposes only.

Following is an example of the classification of one control measure for a pasteurizer installed in a dairy plant.

Selected control measure	Is it feasible for validation?	Does reliability in its effectiveness require frequent monitoring?	Is it intended to control the likelihood of introducing a hazard into the process environment or into the product itself?	Does the effectiveness of other control measures depend on its effectiveness against the identified hazard?	Classification
Milk Pasteurizer	Yes. Pasteurizers are subject to validation, and several parameters have to be defined to ensure the elimination of pathogenic organisms (temperature, time, flow, etc.)	Yes. Pasteurizers required frequent monitoring (most of the time continuously).	No. Pasteurizers are not intended to control the likelihood of introducing hazards. This equipment is used to eliminate the pathogenic organisms contained in raw milk.	No. No other control measures depend on the pasteurizer.	CCP

Table 10 – Example of the classification of a control measure (pasteurizer).

The following table could be the classification for an electronic bottle inspector in a glass container manufacturing plant.

Selected control measure	Is it feasible for validation?	Does reliability in its effectiveness require frequent monitoring?	Is it intended to control the likelihood of introducing a hazard into the process environment or into the product itself?	Does the effectiveness of other control measures depend on its effectiveness against the identified hazard?	Classification
Electronic bottle inspector	Yes. Electronic bottle inspectors are subject to validation. So, the device must be adjusted. The setting of the equipment has to be configured to allow the images captured to be processed appropriately in order to compare shapes and shadows to identify critical defects that could represent hazards.	Yes. Electronic bottle inspectors require frequent monitoring to ensure they are working properly.	No. Electronic bottle inspectors are used to eliminate inherent defects in bottles that could represent physical hazards.	No. No other control measures depend on the electronic bottle inspector.	CCP

Table 11 – Example of the classification of a control measure (electronic bottle inspector).

The next table might be the classification of one control measure for a food manufacturer (a brewing company or a soft drink bottling company) for the same food safety hazard (glass fragments).

Selected control measure	Is it feasible for validation?	Does reliability in its effectiveness require frequent monitoring?	Is it intended to control the likelihood of introducing a hazard into the process environment or into the product itself?	Does the effectiveness of other control measures depend on its effectiveness against the identified hazard?	Classification
Glass breakage procedure	Yes. It is a common practice to determine the number of bottles that must be removed in correlating proximity to the valve where the burst occurred.	Yes. The monitoring activity should be performed every time a glass bottle explodes. In some automatic equipment, other checks must be performed at a very high frequency.	Yes. This control measure is intended to prevent glass fragments from falling inside uncovered bottles within the filler.	—	OPRP

Table 12 – Example of the classification of a control measure (glass breakage procedure).

Metal detectors installed at the end of the line in food manufacturing plants are usually classified as follows:

Selected control measure	Is it feasible for validation?	Does reliability in its effectiveness require frequent monitoring?	Is it intended to control the likelihood of introducing a hazard into the process environment or into the product itself?	Does the effectiveness of other control measures depend on its effectiveness against the identified hazard?	Classification
Metal detector	Yes. Metal detectors are subject to validation. Several important parameters must be considered, including water content in the product, sensitivity settings, speed line, mineral content in the product, test at the center of the aperture, etc.	Yes. Metal detectors usually have to be monitored frequently to ensure they are working properly.	No. This control measure is intended to detect and eliminate metal fragments that might be present in the product either from ingredients or from processing equipment.	No. No other control measures depend on the metal detector.	CCP

Table 13 – Example of the classification of a control measure (metal detector).

Following is an example of the classification of a control measure in raw material receiving:

Selected control measure	Is it feasible for validation?	Does reliability in its effectiveness require frequent monitoring?	Is it intended to control the likelihood of introducing a hazard into the process environment or into the product itself?	Does the effectiveness of other control measures depend on its effectiveness against the identified hazard?	Classification
Antibiotic test during raw milk receiving.	No. Antibiotic test during milk receiving could be considered a verification activity because the acceptable level of the hazard (presence of antibiotics) is directly measured. This hazard is homogeneously distributed in the milk tanks.	—	—	—	PRP. This should also be addressed in the verification plan and included in the management of purchased materials programme (PRP)

Table 14. Example of the classification of a control measure (antibiotic test on milk receiving).

Three terms commonly confused in food safety organizations are defined and clarified below:

Monitoring[2]	*Conducting a planned sequence of observations or measurements to assess whether control measures are operating as intended.*
Verification[2]	*Confirmation, through the provision of objective evidence, that specified requirements have been fulfilled.*
Validation[2]	*<Food Safety> Obtaining evidence that the control measures managed by the HACCP plan by the operational PRP(s) are capable of being effective. This definition is based on the codex and is more suitable for the field of food safety than the definition given in ISO 9000.*

As mentioned before, these definitions alone do not clarify the concepts. The definition of "monitoring" is practically the same as the one provided in the Codex:

Monitor[1] **(verb)**	*The act of conducting a planned sequence of observations or measurements of control parameters to assess whether a CCP is under control.*

It is interesting that ISO-9000:2005 (Quality Management Systems – Fundamentals and Vocabulary) never defined this term, not even in its previous versions. Fortunately, a definition is provided for this term in one of the supporting documents of ISO (ISO/TC 176/SC 1/N 339).

Monitoring[15]	Observe and check over a period of time; maintain regular close observation over.

The term "verification" is taken as is from ISO-9000:2005.

Finally, the term "validation" defined in the standard is exclusive to food safety; yet, it does not vary greatly from the definition provided in ISO-9000:2005.

Validation[8]	Confirmation, through the provision of objective evidence, that the requirements for a specific intended use or application have been fulfilled. Note 1: The term "validated" is used to designate the corresponding status. Note 2: The used conditions for validation can be real or simulated.

In fact, ISO-15161:2001 (guidelines on the application of ISO-9001 for the food and drink industry) provides several examples of processes in food manufacturing that require validation:

- Pasteurizers
- Sterilization in canning
- CIP cleaning

The following figure illustrates the methodology applied in 7.4.3 and 7.4.4 (evaluation and classification of control measures) and also shows how it can be used in two decision trees (figures 20 and 23).

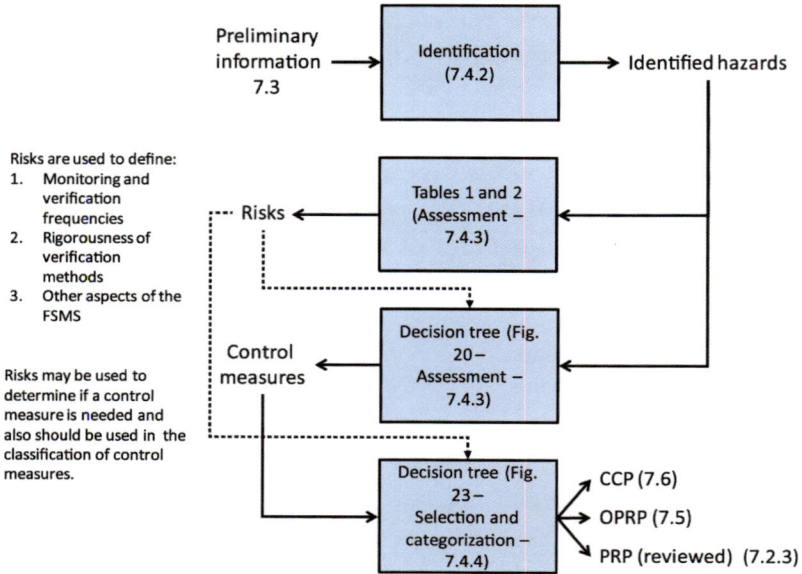

Figure 24 – Decision tree for ISO-22000:2005.

The result of the hazard analysis is the HACCP plan (7.6) and/ or the OPRP (7.5); generally, both are similar documents. The main difference between these two control measures is that OPRP does not identify critical limits.

The following figure illustrates the interactions of the hazard analysis requirements (7.4):

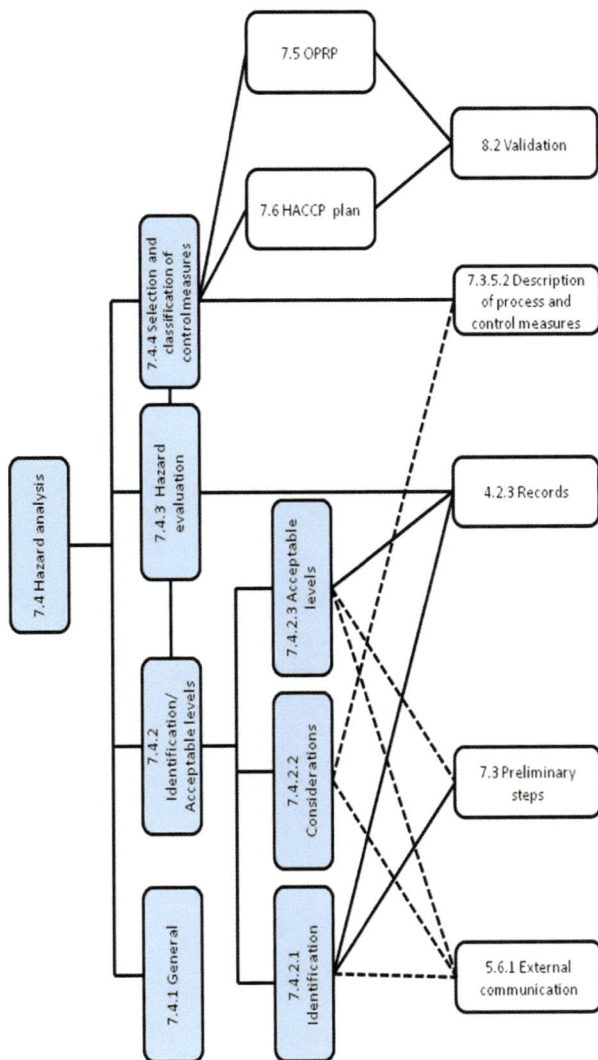

Figure 25 – Interrelationship diagram. Hazard analysis.

Operational Prerequisite Programmes (7.5) and HACCP Plan (7.6)

Before exploring this topic, it is important to review the definition of the quality plan mentioned in ISO-9000:2005.

Quality Plan[8]	*Document specifying which procedures and associated resources shall be applied by whom and when to a specific project, product, process or contract.*

It is a common mistake to refer to the entire hazard analysis as the "HACCP plan." In reality, the HACCP plan is the result of the hazard analysis (as well as the OPRPs and the verification plan), which links activities, responsibilities, frequencies, documents, records methods, and so on.

Compare the definition previously quoted with clauses 7.5 (OPRP) and 7.6.1 (HACCP plan).

7.5 Establishing the operational prerequisite programmes

The operational PRP(s) shall be documented and shall include the following information for each programme:

(a) Food safety hazard(s) to be controlled by the programme (see 7.4.4)
(b) Control Measure(s) (see 7.4.4)
(c) Monitoring procedures that demonstrate that the operational PRP(s) are implemented
(d) Corrections and corrective actions to be taken if monitoring shows that the operational PRP(s) are not in control (see 7.10.1 and 7.10.2, respectively)
(e) Responsibilities and authorities
(f) Record(s) of monitoring

7.6 Establishing the HACCP plan

The HACCP plan shall be documented and shall include the following information for each identified critical control point (CCP):

(a) Food safety hazard(s) to be controlled at the CCP (see 7.4.4)
(b) Control measure(s) (see 7.4.4)
(c) Critical limit(s) (see 7.6.3)
(d) Monitoring procedure(s) (see 7.6.4)
(e) Corrections and corrective action(s) to be taken if critical limits are exceeded (see 7.6.5)
(f) Responsibilities and authorities
(g) Record(s) of monitoring

Both fragments are practically the same with the single exception that critical limits are not necessarily included in the OPRP. Everything else is much the same, a similarity evident in the following excerpt from ISO/TS-22004:2005:

The development of the operational PRP(s) may follow the design of the HACCP plan (see 7.6.1 of ISO 22000:2005).

There are organizations that implement both OPRP(s) and HACCP plans in the same document, even in the quality plan for those companies that already have ISO-9001:2008 implemented.

Critical Limits

According to the standard, a critical limit is defined as follows:

Critical Limit[2]	*Criterion which separates acceptability from unacceptability. Note: Critical limits are established to determine whether a CCP remains in control. If a critical limit is exceeded or violated, the products affected are deemed to be potentially unsafe.*

When a critical limit is exceeded, the resulting product is potentially unsafe, which means it cannot be proven that such a product is safe for use or consumption.

The critical limit determination is linked to the validation of the critical control point (see 8.2); therefore, the same validation record is commonly used to document the rationale for the selection of such critical limits.

Requirements related to the monitoring system as well as corrections and corrective actions taken when a deviation occurs are applicable for the OPRP (7.5) as well as for the CCP (7.6).

The classification of control measures is always a significant debate in the sector. Please consider this list during classification, implementation, and assessment.

PRP(s):

- Must be verified (7.8 – a) and included in the verification plan.
- Food safety team may initiate corrections/corrective actions if verification activities on PRP(s) do not demonstrate conformity with planned arrangements (8.4.2).

OPRP(s):

- Must be monitored (7.5 – c).
- Corrections and corrective actions must be initiated if the monitoring system of the OPRP indicates a loss of control (7.5 – d). (If, after an OPRP failure, it is not possible to start a corrective action [elimination of the problem at the source of the nonconformity], the control measure cannot be classified as OPRP.)
- If a product was manufactured under conditions where OPRP(s) were not conformed, the deviation shall be evaluated with respect to the cause(s) of the nonconformity and to the consequences thereof in terms of food safety and shall, where necessary, be handled as potentially unsafe products (7.10.1).
- Must be verified (7.8 – c)
- Must be validated (8.2).

- Food safety team may initiate corrections/corrective actions if verification activities on OPRP(s) do not demonstrate conformity with planned arrangements (8.4.2).

CCP(s):

- Must be monitored (7.6.4).
- Corrections and corrective actions must be initiated if the monitoring system of the CCP indicates the critical limit was exceeded (7.6.5). (If, after a critical limit is exceeded, it is not possible to start a corrective action [elimination of the problem at the source of the nonconformity], the control measure cannot be classified as CCP.)
- To classify a control measure as a CCP, it must have critical limit(s) (7.6.3).
- If a product was manufactured under conditions where critical limits have been exceeded, that product will be a potentially unsafe product (7.10.1).
- Must be verified (7.8 – c)
- Must be validated (8.2).
- Food safety team may initiate corrections/corrective actions if verification activities on CCPs do not demonstrate conformity with planned arrangements (8.4.2).

Updating of Preliminary Information (7.7)

Once the HACCP plan and the OPRP are documented and implemented, the organization will update all preliminary information (if necessary). The update is necessary in those cases where modifications have been made after the hazard analysis and the implementation of the HACCP plan and/or the OPRP. It is important to leave evidence of this activity in a food safety team meeting record.

Verification Plan (7.8)

It is really common to see weaknesses on verification planning. The verification plan can take the HACCP plan format as long as it establishes the following:

- Purpose
- Method
- Frequencies
- Responsibilities
- Records

This applies to verification activities related to the following:

- Prerequisite programmes (all)
- Input to the hazard analysis
- OPRP effectiveness
- HACCP plan effectiveness
- Acceptable levels
- Other aspects

The requirements related to verification activities in this standard suggest a dependable system.

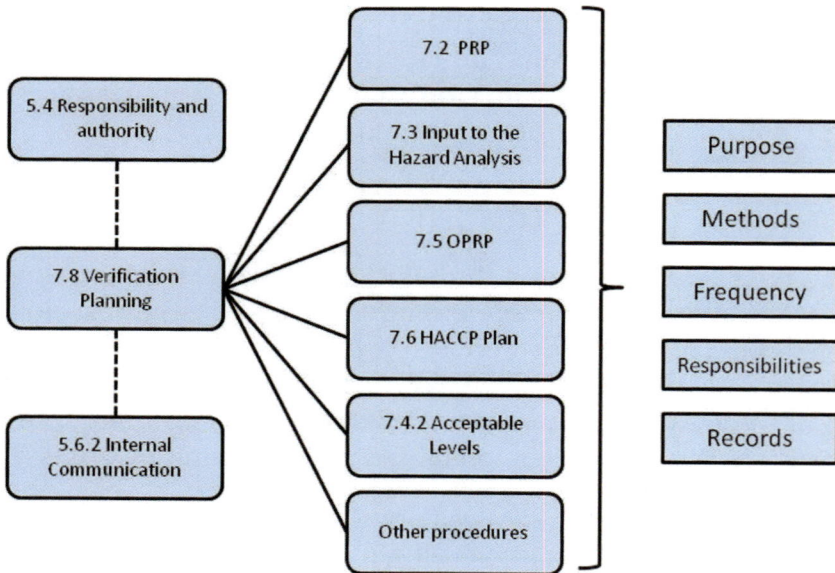

Figure 26 – Interrelationship diagram. Verification planning.

The planning section of ISO-22000:2005 was explained in a diagram similar to figure 27 in one of the drafts of the standard in 2004. The figure was updated, and the twelve Codex steps are signaled by circles along with the clause numbers of the standard signaled by boxes.

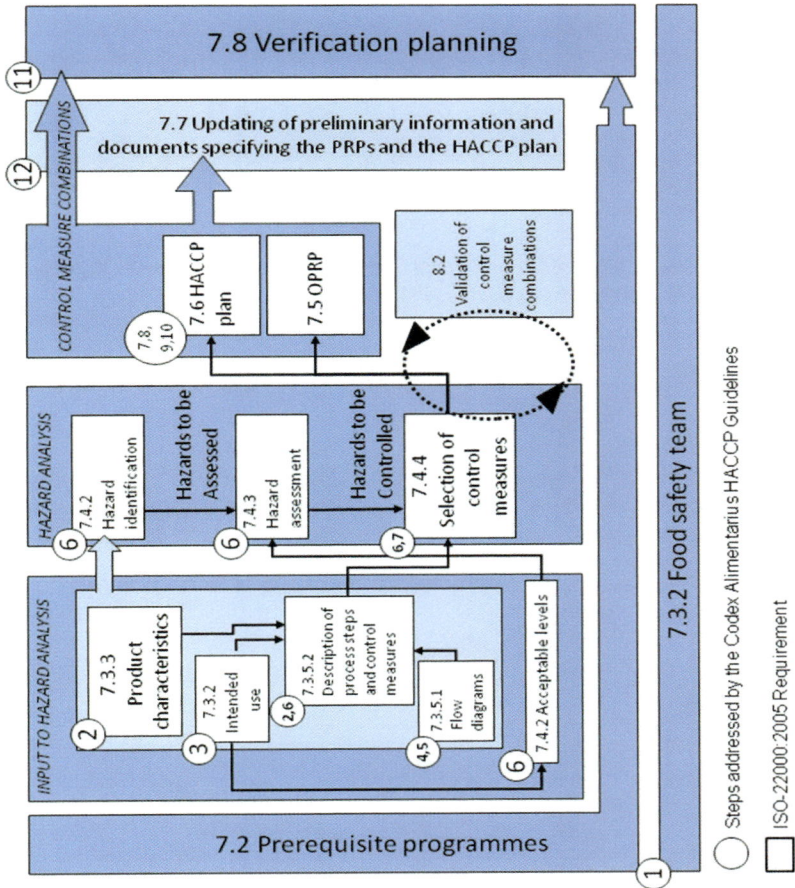

Figure 27 – Planning steps in ISO-22000:2005 (adapted from ISO/ DIS-22000:2004).

Category J (transport and storage). Orange juice transportation on liquid nitrogen in Veracruz, Mexico. Photo by Cesar Ramirez.

Traceability (7.9)

The organization shall establish and apply a traceability system that enables the identification of product lots and their relation to batches of raw materials, processing and delivery records.

The definition for traceability in ISO-9000:2005 is as follows:

Traceability[8]	*Ability to trace the history, application or location of that which is under consideration.*

ISO-22005:2007 (Traceability in the feed and food chain – General principles and basic requirements for system design and implementation) provides a more appropriate definition for the sector:

Traceability[11]	Ability to follow the movement of a feed or food through specified stage(s) of production, processing and distribution.

ISO-22000:2005 clearly determines where an organization's traceability system begins and ends.

The traceability system shall be able to identify incoming material from the immediate suppliers and the initial distribution route of the end product.

Lot[11]	Set of units of a product which have been produced and/or processed or packaged under similar circumstances.
Lot Identification[11]	Process of assigning a unique code to a lot.
Location[11]	Place of production, processing, distribution, storage and handling from primary production to consumption.

ISO-22005:2007 establishes these important conditions for the traceability system review:

Traceability test results
Traceability audit findings
Changes to product or processes

Traceability-related information provided by other organizations in the feed and food chain
Corrective actions related to traceability
Customer feedback, including complaints, related to traceability
New or amended regulations affecting traceability
New statistical evaluation methods

Control of Nonconformities (7.10)

The ISO-22000:2005 standard classifies the status of a product in the following way (note: these are not official definitions):

Nonconforming Product:
    A product that after being previously considered a potentially unsafe product and did not meet any of the criteria in the evaluation mentioned in 7.10.3.2. There are only two permissible dispositions for these products:

> *(a) Reprocessing or further processing within or outside the organization to ensure that the food safety hazard is eliminated or reduced to acceptable levels*
> *(b) Destruction and /or disposal as waste*

Potentially Unsafe Product:
    Product resulting in the failure of a control measure classified as a CCP or OPRP. It is not certain that the product is safe for use or consumption. These products require a further evaluation (7.10.3.2) to determine their disposition. It is possible that within an organization, someone with certain responsibility and authority can deem a product as potentially unsafe for different causes mentioned in this same paragraph.

Corrections (7.10.1) and Corrective Actions (7.10.2)

Some organizations confuse corrections and corrective actions and use them interchangeably. In fact, it is still common to see HACCP plans that refer to corrections as corrective actions. ISO-15161:2001 takes care to emphasize the difference:

The concept of corrective action in the HACCP method describes the processing of nonconforming products and the nonconformities and the correction of the situation. The concept of corrective action in ISO 9001 is based on searching for causes in such a way as to perpetuate the elimination of the problem at the source of the nonconformity.

Correction[2]	*Action to eliminate a detected nonconformity. For the purposes of this International Standard, a correction relates to the handling of potentially unsafe products, and can therefore be made in conjunction with a corrective action.*
CorrectiveAction[2]	*Action to eliminate the cause of a detected nonconformity or other undesirable situation. Corrective action includes cause analysis and is taken to prevent recurrence.*

Clause 7.10.1 (corrections) gives a pattern to determine whether the failure was in a CCP or in an OPRP; these differences are further explained in figures 28 and 29.

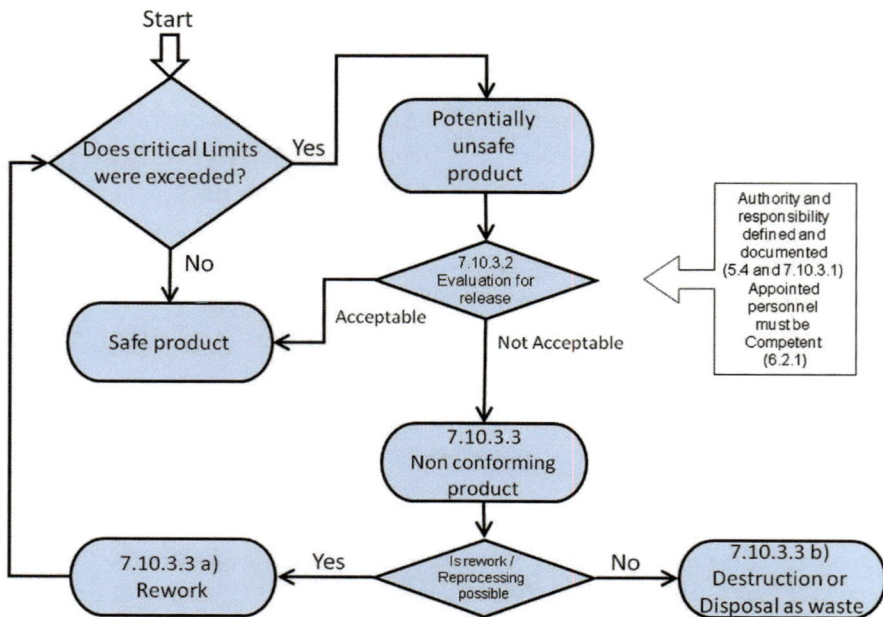

Figure 28 – Actions to be considered when a critical limit is exceeded.

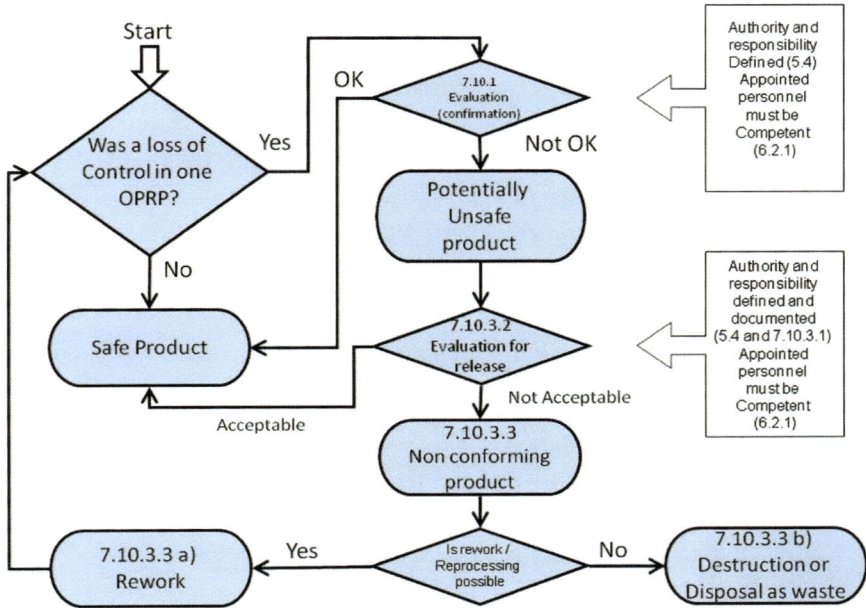

Figure 29 – Actions to be considered when an OPRP has a loss of control.

The most important difference in the responses that are permitted when critical limits are exceeded, or when an OPRP has a loss of control, is in this last case (only a previous evaluation by qualified staff and assigned responsibility); once such loss of control is detected, it is decided whether the affected product will be considered potentially unsafe. In the first scenario (CCP failure), the manufactured product—where the critical limit was exceeded—will automatically be a pottenctially unsafe product.

This is the source of the previous two figures (28 and 29):

Products manufactured under conditions where critical limits have been exceeded are potentially unsafe products and shall be handled in accordance with 7.10.3.

Products manufactured under conditions where operational PRP(s) have not been conformed with shall be evaluated with respect to the cause(s) of the nonconformity and to the consequences thereof in terms of food safety and shall, where necessary, be handled in accordance with 7.10.3.

A documented procedure will be established for both corrections and corrective actions. Generally, the first one is integrated with the nonconforming product procedure when ISO-22000:2005 integrates with ISO-9001:2008. The corrective actions are an essential part of any management system and should be used (as it is mentioned in its definition) to eliminate the cause of detected nonconformities or any undesired situation. The following figure lists some triggers for corrective actions.

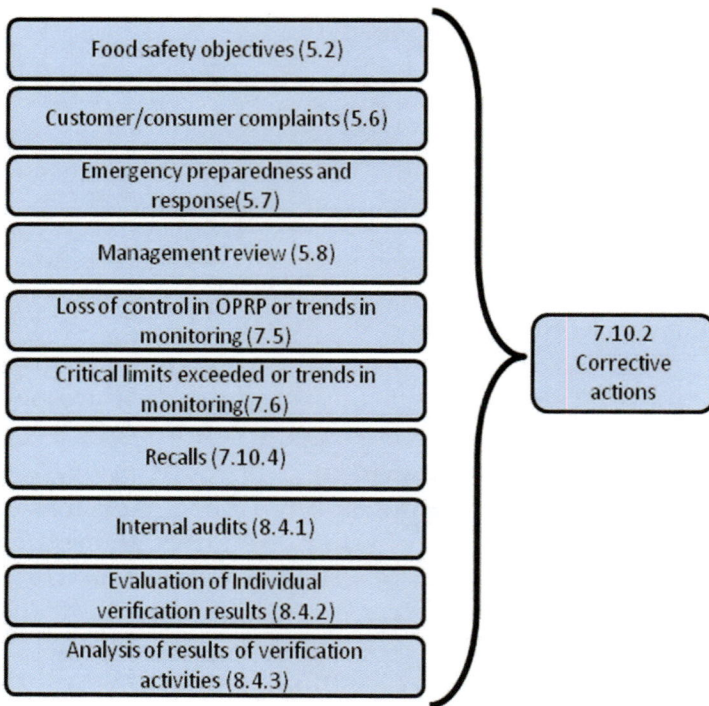

```
Food safety objectives (5.2)
Customer/consumer complaints (5.6)
Emergency preparedness and response(5.7)
Management review (5.8)
Loss of control in OPRP or trends in monitoring (7.5)
Critical limits exceeded or trends in monitoring(7.6)                    7.10.2
Recalls (7.10.4)                                                       Corrective
Internal audits (8.4.1)                                                  actions
Evaluation of Individual verification results (8.4.2)
Analysis of results of verification activities (8.4.3)
```

Figure 30 – Corrective actions. Common triggers.

The following interrelationship diagram demonstrates the links between the requirements in 7.10 and the standard's other requirements. The diagram reveals the relationships that develop when a lack of control exists in OPRP(s) and/or in the CCPs as well as the links with responsibility and authority (5.4) and competence (6.2.2).

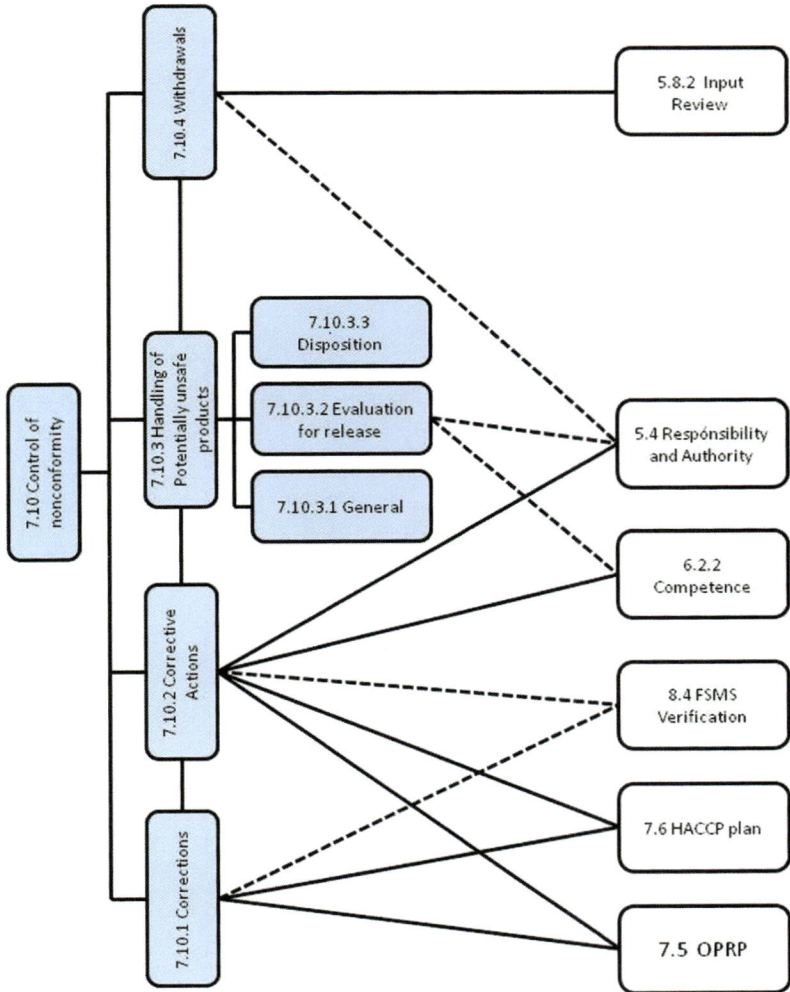

Figure 31 – Interrelationship diagram. Control of nonconformities.

Handling of Potentially Unsafe Products (7.10.3)

The upper part of figure 31 illustrates the relationships that exist in the requirements of 7.10 in four main sections: Corrections, Corrective actions, Handling of potentially unsafe products, and Withdrawals with important activities related to the control of nonconformities.

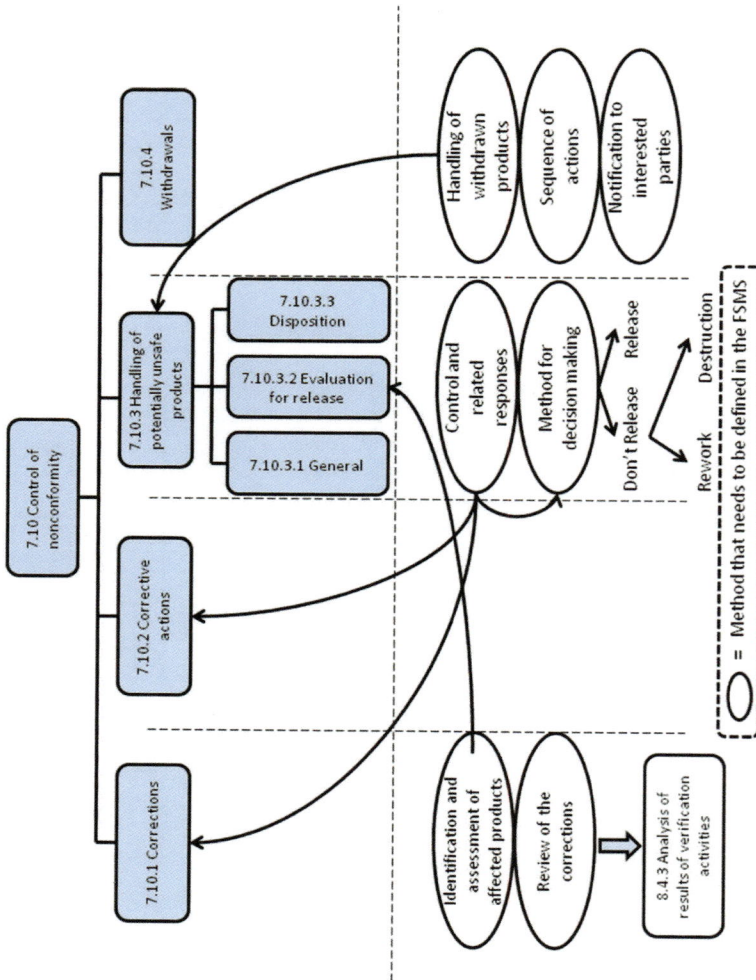

Figure 32 – Interrelationship diagram. Control of nonconformities (part 2).

Withdrawals (7.10.4)

The organization must be prepared to withdraw products that were determined unsafe after any failure in the FSMS and when it is out of control of the organization.

This requires a documented procedure. The procedure must include

> *(1) Notification to relevant interested parties (e.g. statutory and regulatory authorities, customers and/or consumers*
> *(2) Handling of withdrawn products as well as affected lots of the products still in stock, and*
> *(3) The sequence of actions to be taken*

Because of the emphasis on verification activities, the standard can also ask the organization to verify the efficiency of the withdrawal program through an acceptable method.

> *The organization shall verify and record the effectiveness of the withdrawal programme through the use of appropriate techniques (e.g. mock withdrawal or practice withdrawal).*

In section five, the importance of external communication in any organization within the food chain was mentioned. Regarding withdrawals, communication takes on a crucial role.

The following points must be considered by organizations that provide products for other organizations within the food chain when communicating a withdrawal:

- The notification will clarify only the quantity of the affected product, including both the quantity the client has as well as inventory. Therefore, lot numbers will be included. It is important for the client to perceive that the organization has records of the affected delivered lots and a solid traceability system.

- Include that other products the clients might have are not affected and why. At this point, it is important to communicate in a way that will not leave interested parties in doubt about other products that are about to be used or consumed.
- Explain the nature of the problem and its possible consequences to the customer and/or consumers. It is important to be precise and honest in order to avoid underestimating possible severe problems.
- Give a brief explanation about how the problem was detected. As long as the situation is confirmed, never communicate incomplete or unsustainable conclusions.
- Provide the name, phone number, and e-mail of someone he or she can contact immediately upon receiving news of the product in question.

For those organizations that sell, distribute, or manufacture products that go out to consumers and are required to give a statement of a withdrawal to the public, it is important to consider the following:

- Include pictures and/or copies of labels of the affected product in the statement with the purpose of facilitating the identification of the product for the consumer.
- Include the affected lot numbers, the location of the lots in the product (preferably with a picture), and places where the product was distributed.
- Explain the nature of the problem and the possible consequences for the consumer (if possible, explain symptoms that the consumer might have).
- Offer the name of someone to contact by phone and e-mail.

Many times the survival of an organization within a food chain after a withdrawal depends heavily on how honestly and directly the situation is handled.

Category K (equipment manufacturing). Manufacturing of two sanitary tanks for fryer oil storage for a french fry processor. Photo courtesy of Charlottetown Metal Products.

8. – Validation, Verification, and System Improvement

Validation of Control Measures (8.2)

Validations are made before the implementation or after any change. The control measures that are managed with the HACCP plan, and the operational prerequisite programmes (OPRP) are subject to validation. Accepted methods for the validation of the control measures are included in ISO/TS-22004:2005:

(a) *Reference to validations carried out by others, to scientific literature, or to historical knowledge*
(b) *Experimental trials to simulate process conditions*
(c) *Biological, chemical and physical hazard data collected during normal operating conditions*
(d) *Statistically designed surveys*
(e) *Mathematical modeling*
(f) *Use of a guide approved by competent authorities*

These can be used by themselves or in combination.

The objective of a validation is to show that a control measure is capable of eliminating or decreasing an identified hazard to an acceptable level.

The following form is proposed for the realization of these validations.

Control Measure	
Location	

Initial Validation ☐   Re-validation ☐

Approach (thick the approach[es] that apply)

		Justification of the selected approach
Scientific References		
Industry Guidelines		
Previous validation studies		
On-site test		
Data collection		
Mathematical modeling		
Other (explain)		

Decision parameters/Validation acceptance criteria

Hazard(s) to be controlled	
Variables to consider	
Possible limitations	
Criteria for re-validation / Partial validation	
Design of experiments	
Expected results	

Conditions in which validation was performed

Environmental conditions	
Line speed / other process parameters	
Product(s)	

Results

Attach details. Document the criteria for the selection of the critical limits.

Acceptable ☐   Not-acceptable ☐

Calibration (8.3)

For a control measure to be reliable, any measuring device should be properly calibrated to ensure that the measurements obtained are precise. Strictly regarding ISO-22000:2005, only equipment and devices used for monitoring control measures would be in the calibration program. Errors related to calibration include the following:

- Measuring equipment was calibrated out of the range use, where the equipment operates without covering the critical limit of a CCP.
- One or more validations were performed in a CCP or an OPRP with an instrument that was not calibrated, or such information was not included in the validation record.
- There was not an evaluation record of the validity of the previous measurement resulting when the equipment or process was found not to conform to requirements.

Category L ([bio]chemicals). Cleaning agents manufacturing site in Coahuila, Mexico. Photo by Hector Siller.

Food Safety Management System Verification
Internal Audits (8.4.1)

Internal audits are part of the management system verification. The requirements are practically the same as in ISO-9001:2008. Internal audits in the FSMS represent part of the verification system. The main difference between an internal audit and a verification activity in an organization is that the first one has to be made by a person independent of the activity being audited.

Audit[6]	*Systematic, independent and documented process for obtaining audit evidence and evaluating it objectively to determine the extent to which audit criteria are fulfilled.*

During the implementation of any management system one of the most important yet difficult elements to implement is the internal audits. Having deficient internal audits can create a false sense of security or can complicate the management system making it more bureaucratic (preparing unnecessary documentation to correct irrelevant findings) and therefore unsustainable.

The audit planning requirement is to consider the importance of the processes and use the results of previous audit to schedule the internal audits. This is asking you to apply a risk based approach; to focus on areas, activities and processes where problems are likely to occur; and areas where a failure can have serious consequences.

A common failure in audit programs is having auditors using only checklists and verifying compliance with procedures. Those activities are normal during an audit but it shouldn't be the only focus. Internal auditors are more familiar with their organization than any other external auditor and they should verify all aspects of the food safety management system to confirm its effectiveness. This may include:

- Verifying the traceability information
- Assessing the monitoring systems of CCPs and OPRPs (confirming monitoring activities are performed by competent personnel, verifying actions after a failure, confirming the verification activities are carried out appropriately, etc.)
- Considering relevant information to center the audit on specific areas of concern using previous audit results, consumer/customer complaints, previous recalls, the results of the analysis of verification activities, trends on potentially unsafe products, results of regulatory inspections or customer audits, new ingredients).

One key for an effective FSMS is having competent internal auditors. Internal Audits are a crucial aspect to ensure the implementation of the FSMS. Management should use the audit results to ensure the effectiveness and sustainability of FSMS.

Evaluation of Individual Verification Results and Analysis of Results of Verification Activities (8.4.2, 8.4.3)

The following figure (33) shows the relationships of the evaluation of verification results. The results of the verification plan are periodically evaluated to implement corrections and corrective actions when necessary.

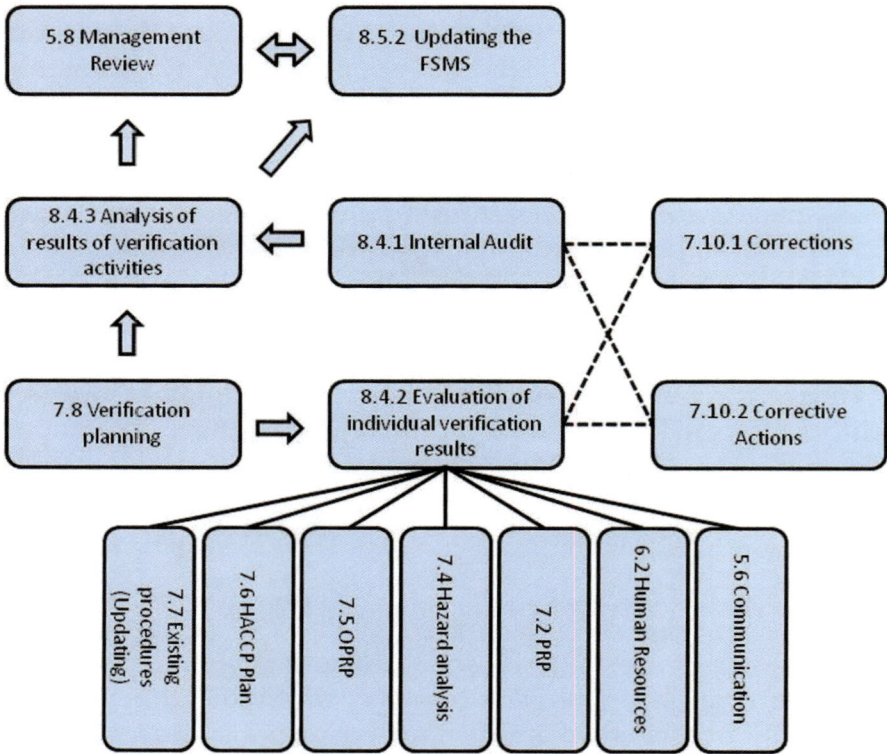

Figure 33 – Interrelationship diagram. FSMS verification system.

At planned intervals, usually prior to the management review, the food safety team will conduct an analysis of the result of verification activities. The input information for such analyses are the audit results (internal and external) and those from the verification plan.

In the cross-references of the standard against ISO-9001, notice that the data analysis is equivalent to the verification activities analysis (8.4.3).

Information [8]	*Meaningful data.*

The expected results of this analysis are clearly mentioned in the standard and are as follows:

(a) To confirm that the overall performance of the system meets the planned arrangements and the Food Safety Management System requirements established by the organization

(b) To identify the need for updating or improving the Food Safety Management System

(c) To identify trends which indicate a higher incidence of potentially unsafe products

(d) To establish information for planning of the internal audit programme concerning the status and importance of areas to be audited and

(e) To provide evidence that any corrections and corrective actions that have been taken are effective.

This clause is sometimes inappropriately addressed in a management system, an oversight that can lead to a superficial analysis or information that does not show or indicate any substance.

The analysis of the results of verification activities should be considered a viewpoint from the food safety team regarding the performance of the verification tools of the FSMS; it is the basis for relevant decisions in the management review (5.8) and the system update (8.5.2). Analyses of verification results will typically include the following:

- Provide the opinion of the food safety team about the compliance related to the planned arrangements
- Emphasize areas of opportunity within the management system
- Emphasize processes and/or activities in risk as well as processes and/or activities that are considered robust
- Alert about monitoring tendencies that can lead to a loss of control in OPRP and/or CCP and provide actions to revert them

- Provide a base for the next internal audit program
- Provide possible topics related to training needs
- Confirm the effectiveness of corrections and corrective actions triggered from failures in control measures

One of the most common failures in an FSMS is a superficial verification system (including internal audits). These are typically recognized by the following:

- PRP verifications with invariable or inflexible frequencies and rigorousness that does not consider important circumstances such as new employees, the presence of contractors for a specific project, new installations and services, etc.
- Internal audits based only on checklists (a checklist should be only one of several tools used by internal auditors)
- Managers who emphasize compliance with established verification frequencies rather than the correction of deficiencies found
- Internal audits or verifications to confirm compliance in document control, calibration, training schedules, and other isolated activities
- Internal audit records with reported deficiencies that are ambiguous and do not assist the auditee to understand the detected failures or gaps
- Internal auditors who focus only on compliance with the standard instead of identifying areas of risk and improvement opportunities

Improvement (8.5)

Continual Improvement[8]	Recurring activity to increase the ability to fulfill requirements.

Like any management system standard, ISO-22000:2005 also has a clause (8.5.1) regarding improvement.

Top management shall ensure that the organization continually improves the effectiveness of the Food Safety Management System through the use of
Communication (see 5.6),
Management review (see 5.8),
Internal audit (see 8.4.1),
Evaluation of individual verification results (see 8.4.2),
Analysis of results of verification activities (see 8.4.3),
Validation of control measure combinations (see 8.2),
Corrective actions (see 7.10.2), and
Food Safety Management System updating (see 8.5.2).

The standard highlights elements that are linked to improvement. There is another important element: food safety objectives. In the following figure (34), it is obvious that within these listed elements there are four phases found in the management system cycle (plan, do, check, and act).

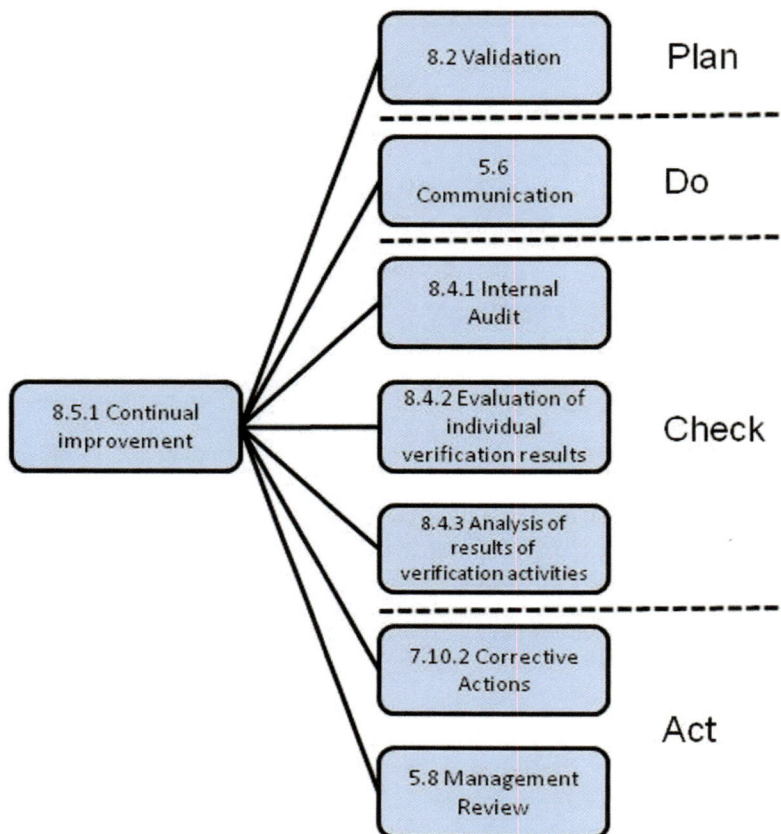

Figure 34 – Interrelationship diagram.
Continuous improvement and PDCA cycle.

Updating[2]	Immediate and/or planned activity to ensure application of the most recent information.

It is common for clause 8.5.2 (Updating the food safety management system) to be confused with clause 7.7 (Updating of preliminary information and documents). The main difference here is that the last clause mainly refers to the preliminary steps to enable hazard analysis (7.3) and is generally an activity that is not always cyclical.

Updating the FSMS is a cyclic activity and should be defined in the FSMS with an emphasized link to the management review and the analysis of results of verification activities, as shown in figure 33.

The elements to evaluate within the system update are included, along with possible examples to consider:

- Communication (external and internal): consumer/client complaints, inspection reports from government agencies and/or other interested parties, new customer requirements, regulation changes, proposed industry guides and recommended codes of practice, changes in services, and other factors.
- Other information: information related to methods/validation records of control measures, new technology or equipment, possible potential emergency situations, food safety objectives, and so forth.
- Output of the analysis of verification activities: the result of the application from clause 8.4.3 mentioned in this section.
- Management review results mentioned in section five.

The expected result in the FSMS update is mentioned in the same clause, although figure 35 displays the same information in a clearer manner.

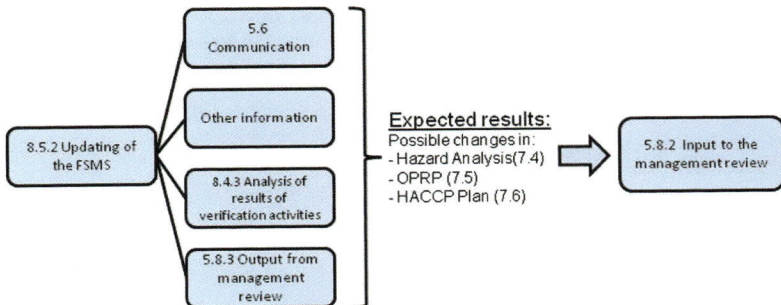

Figure 35 – Interrelationship diagram. Updating the FSMS.

Figure 35 describes the relationship between clause 8.5.1 (Continual improvement) and 8.5.2 (Updating of the FSMS).

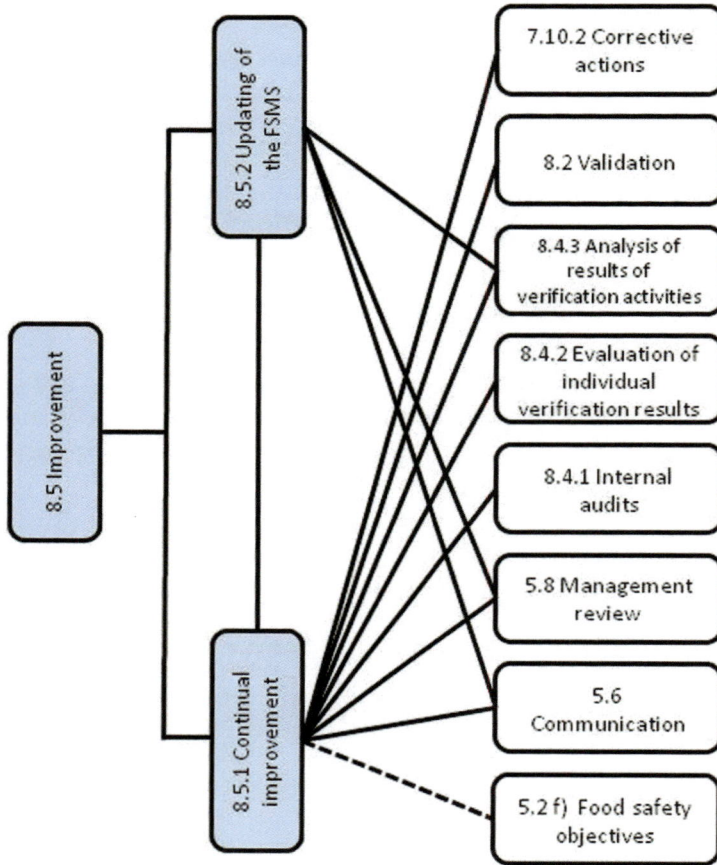

Figure 36 – Interrelationship diagram. Continuous improvement.

The explanation of the requirements ends here. It is important to conclude with one reminder: the standard ISO-22000:2005 is a document with interrelated requirements that can be completely understood as all of its interrelationships are mastered.

I hope that this will be a useful, frequently consulted guide.

Category M. Glass bottle manufacturing in San Luis Potosi, Mexico. Photo by Juan Rivera.

9. – Notes

1. CAC/RCP 1969 Rev. 4, 2003 International Code of Recommended Practices for the General Principles of Hygiene Products.

2. ISO-22000:2005 Food Safety Management Systems – Requirements for any organization in the food chain (2005-09-01).

3. ISO/FDIS-22000:2005 Food Safety Management Systems – Requirements for any organization in the food chain (Final Draft) (2005-03-04).

4. ISO/DIS-22000:2004 Food Safety Management Systems – Requirements for any organization throughout the food chain (Draft International Standard) (2004-06-03).

5. ISO/TS-22004:2005 Food Safety Management System – Guidance on the application of ISO-22000:2005 (2005-11-15).

6. ISO/PDTS-22004 Food Safety Management System – Guidance on the use of ISO-22000:2005 (Working Draft) (2005-05-31).

7. ISO/PDTS-22004 Food Safety Management System – Guidance on the use of ISO-22000:2005 (2004-12-17) (Working Draft).

8. ISO-9000:2005 Quality Management Systems – Foundations and Vocabulary.

9. ISO-9001:2008 Quality Management Systems – Requirements.

10. ISO-15161:2001 Guidelines on the application of ISO-9001:2000 for the food and drink industry (2001-11-15).

11. ISO-22005:2007 Traceability in the feed and food chain – General principles and basic requirements for system design and implementation.

12. PAS-220:2208 Specification of common management system requirements as a framework for integration (Now ISO/ TS-22002-1:2009).

13. CAC/GL 69-2008 Guidelines for the Validation of Food Safety Control Measures.

14. PAS-99:2006 Specification of common management system requirements as a framework for integration.

15. ISO/TC 176/SC 2/N 526R2 ISO-9000 Introduction and Support Package: Guidance on the Terminology Used in ISO 9001and ISO 9004.

16. ISO/TS-22003:2007 Food Safety Management Systems – Requirements for bodies providing audit and certification of Food Safety Management Systems.

17. ISO 9001 Auditing Practices Group Guidance on: Auditing 'competence' and the 'effectiveness of actions taken.'

18. ISO-22000 Food Safety Management System. An easy-to-use checklist for small business. Are you ready?/The International Trade Center and ISO. 2008.

19. ISO Guide 72 on justification and drafting of management system standards. Richard de Grood (Philips Medical Systems) and Dick Hortensius (Netherlands Standardization Institute) ISO BULLETIN MARCH 2002.

20. ISO/TC 176/SC 2/N 526R2 ISO 9000. Introduction and Support Package: Guidance on the Terminology Used in ISO 9001and ISO 9004.

10. – Photographs and Credits

ISO/TS-22003:2007 classifies the food chain into thirteen categories:

- Category A Farming 1 (animals). Chicken farm for egg production in Puebla, Mexico. Photo by Jose A. Camacho.
- Category B Farming 2 (plants). Lettuce field in Baja California, Mexico. Photo by the author.
- Category C Processing 1 (perishable animal products). Fish processing in the Bén Tre Province, Vietnam. Photo by Carlos Jaimes.
- Category D Processing 2 (perishable and preserved vegetable products). Aseptic mango juice in Sinaloa, Mexico. Photo by Cesar Ramirez.
- Category E Processing 3 (products with long shelf life). Frozen donut line in Nuevo Leon, Mexico. Photo by Erika Cortez.
- Category F (feed). Fermentation process for feed production in Zhejiang, China. Photo by Henry Turlington.
- Category G (catering). Catering services in Coahuila, Mexico. Photo by Juan R. Cardenas.
- Category H (retail outlets, shops, wholesalers). Vegetable shelves in Baja California, Mexico. Photo by the author.
- Category I (services). Installation and start-up of a specialty packaging line for a Canadian pork processor. Photo courtesy of Charlottetown Metal Products.
- Category J (transport and storage). Orange juice transportation on liquid nitrogen in Veracruz, Mexico. Photo by Cesar Ramirez.

- Category K (equipment manufacturing). Manufacturing of two sanitary tanks for fryer oil storage for a french fry processor. Photo courtesy of Charlottetown Metal Products.
- Category L ([bio]chemicals). Cleaning agents manufacturing site in Coahuila, Mexico. Photo by Hector Siller.
- Category M. Glass bottle manufacturing in San Luis Potosi, Mexico. Photo by Juan Rivera.

II. – Index (definitions)